The Bible! Myth or Message?

I0169511

Michael Penny

ISBN: 978-1-78364-445-2

First Edition published in 1982
Revised Second Edition published 2011
Updated Third Edition published 2018

The Open Bible Trust
Fordland Mount, Upper Basildon,
Reading, RG8 8LU, UK.

www.obt.org.uk

Italics in quotations are generally the author's and are used for emphasis; except in the *King James Version* quotations, where italics indicate 'English words added by the translators, which are not directly in the original-language documents'.

With indented quotations, where appropriate, the quotation marks have been omitted.

****

————————————

The Bible!
Myth or Message?

Contents

Reviews of the First Edition

"This book asks a series of questions. What is the Bible? Where did it come from? Is it unique? Is it fact or fiction? Is it inspired? Is it worth reading? Is it worth studying? Is it worth believing?

As a sub-title the cover advertises the contents the book as 'containing amazing facts about the book Christians call *God's Word.*' Without becoming too technical, the author has assembled facts and arguments attesting the authenticity of the Bible as being a message to mankind from his Creator.

Some of the facts are already well known, others are lesser known, but nevertheless, well worth reading. The main value of the book is that all these proofs of the Bible's origin are brought together in an attractive manner into one volume. Certainly worth having and reading." (Reviewed by Basil D. Varnam in *Redemption Tidings,* UK)

"The author shows that the Bible, far from being discredited by modern knowledge, is still reliable, relevant and the authentic word of God. Many charts and diagrams enhance the liveliness of the text." (Reviewed by *Christian Weekly Newspapers,* UK)

"If you want to reinforce your trust in the uniqueness of the Bible – or need ammunition to use with friends who claim the Bible is merely a book – try Michael Penny's *The Bible – Myth or Message?*" (Reviewed by David Hall in *Family*, UK)

Preface to the Second Edition

The first edition of the book was entitled *The Bible – Myth or Message?* and it went out of print some years ago. A number of people have, over that time, expressed their disappointment at not being able to obtain a copy. I am grateful to all these people, and especially to those who asked for it to be reprinted. And I am especially grateful to those who suggested there should be a second, improved and expanded edition. This I have done. I hope that the changes have made this second edition more readable and understandable, and that the additions have made it a more helpful and more useful book.

I am very indebted to Geoff Wright, not only for his enthusiasm for the first edition and desire for a second edition, but also for all the work he put in scanning and then editing the text of that first edition. This saved me hours of work, and has enabled me to spend more time improving and expanding the content of this second edition. He also compiled the very valuable indexes.

I am also indebted to Brian Sherring and Cliff Richmond, both of whom did excellent work in proof reading and commenting upon the final manuscript.

As with the first edition, our desire and prayer is that this second edition will be used to the glory of God, and will receive a measure of His blessing.

Soli Deo gloria.

MICHAEL PENNY
March 2011

Preface to the First Edition

Various parts of the first draft of this book were tested upon the Christian Fellowship of Queen Mary's Sixth Form College, Basingstoke; the C.Y.F.A. of St. Mary's, Eastrop in Basingstoke; and members of the Christian Union at Lancaster University. The final draft was prepared in the light of their comments and criticisms, and deals with various difficulties and problems experienced in their Christian witness. A sincere thank you is extended to them all.

Frank Peachey has been of the greatest assistance with his most enriching advice and very constructive criticism. Without him this book would have been much poorer and I am deeply grateful for all that he has done.

The desire of all who helped with this book is that it will be used to the glory of God. Our prayer is that it will receive a measure of His blessing.

Soli Deo gloria.

MICHAEL PENNY
January 1982

The Bible!
Myth or Message?

What is the Bible?

Where did it come from?

Is it a collection of ancient myths and stories?

Or a mixture of fact and fiction?

Is it unique?

Is it reliable?

Is it inspired?

Does it contain a message for mankind?

If so – from whom?

Man or God?

Section 1.
The Bible!
A Peculiar Book?
Is It Worth Reading?

The chief knowledge that a man gets from reading books is the knowledge that few of them are worth reading.

(H. L. MENCKEN, 1880-1956)

I fell asleep reading a dull book, and I dreamt I was reading on, so I awoke from sheer boredom.

(HEINRICH HEINE, 1797-1856)

The books that everybody admires are those that nobody reads.

(ANATOLE FRANCE, 1844-1924)

In the main there are two sorts of book, those that no one reads and those that no one ought to read.

(H. L. MENCKEN, 1880-1956)

Most contemporary books give the impression of having been manufactured in a day out of books read the day before.

(NICHOLAS CHAMFORT, 1741-1794)

Setting the Scene – The Past

Until 1384 there was no English translation of the Bible, the main one used being in Latin. Most of those who attempted to learn that language did so for the sole purpose of being able to read the Bible for themselves. To be able to do so was, to them, well worth the problems and difficulties of learning such a strange language.

Several English versions appeared in the next two hundred years. In 1384 John Wycliffe[1] produced the first Bible in English, but as there were no printing presses this was a rather large volume and not readily available and few people could read. The next century, however, saw the invention of the printing press, and in 1525 William Tyndale's translation became the first 'printed' New Testament in English.

The first 'printed' Bible in English was translated by Bishop Miles Coverdale. It appeared in 1535 and was revised in 1539. Archbishop Thomas Cranmer made a further revision in 1540.

1560 saw the publication of the Geneva Bible. This was the first small print Bible, using a Roman font. It also had notes explaining the more obscure passages. This became popular and helped to fuel the reformation and to help the cause of the reformers. The Catholic Church brought out the Douai New Testament in 1582, and the Old Testament followed in 1609. However, this was not a translation from the original Hebrew and Greek, but from the 5th century Latin Vulgate.

King James was quite a scholar and was fluent in Greek and French, and had attempted to translate the Psalms himself. In 1601 he asked the Scottish Kirk to produce a new translation of the Bible, but they rejected his pleas. In 1604 he convened a conference at Hampton Court, to try and

---

[1] We have used the word 'produced' rather than 'translate'. On page 221 of *The Book and the Parchments,* referring to Wycliffe, F. F. Bruce questions "whether he actually did much translation himself" but states that "the work was carried out under his influence and in accordance with his policy."

resolve disputes between the high and low (Puritan) wings of the Church of England. In that he failed, but the conference did agree that a new translation into English was needed.

Forty-seven scholars were appointed, and given permission to borrow from earlier translations, if they thought it appropriate. They scrupulously checked each other's work and completed a final draft in just four years. This was then critically reviewed over the next nine months by scholars from Oxford, Cambridge and Westminster.

The result was, in 1611, the King James Authorized Version (*KJV*) became the accepted Bible in churches and homes. Yet, in most homes people could still neither read nor write. The motivation behind many people wanting to learn to do so was their desire to read the Bible for themselves. To them it was definitely worth reading. To them it was not a book written by men. It was a book written by God. It was God's Word. Such a situation continued for a further two to three hundred years or so, but during the last century things began to change and now ... things have changed completely.

Setting the Scene – The Present

Now that nearly everyone can read, and the Bible is the world's best-selling book, it is perhaps strange that hardly anyone wants to read it and few consider it worth the effort. Previously the person who rejected the Bible was the one who was on the defensive. He had to put his case and justify his actions; but now it is the turn of those who accept the Bible as worthy of reading. Now it is they who are on the defensive and have to state why such a book is of value to the reader. As George puts it in Tom Stoppard's play, *Jumpers:*

Well, the tide is running the atheist's way, and it is a tide which has turned only once in human history ... there is presumably a calendar date – *a moment* – when the onus of proof passed from the atheist to the believer, when, quite suddenly, secretly, the noes had it.

When was that calendar date, that moment in time? We cannot be precise, but the last century saw the tide turn significantly. It had started towards the end of the nineteenth century. By the end of the twentieth, opposition to Christianity and aggressive atheism manifested themselves in a variety of ways. The age of faith was ebbing away fast and was being replaced by several different ideas.

In the second half of the nineteenth century a great deal of attention was being paid to the necessity of education. Educated scholars probed everything with their cautious questioning. These were the rationalists.

> RATIONALISM – The practice of explaining the supernatural in religion in a way consistent with reason, or of treating reason as the ultimate authority in religion as elsewhere. The theory that reason is the foundation of certainty in knowledge.

To them, everything had to be rational, logical and reasonable. This was also when science and scientific method advanced by leaps and bounds. Reason and logic were the foundations, and everything had to be measured. If it couldn't be measured, it didn't exist! Such is still the position of some scientists now, yet one wonders in what units they would measure love! That cannot be measured and it often transcends reason and defies logic; but he who says love does not exist is one who cannot share in the truth expressed by Tennyson, that:

> Tis better to have loved and lost,
> than never to have loved at all.

Also in the last half of the nineteenth century there were the secularists.

> SECULARISM – Concerned with the affairs of the world; worldly, not sacred; not monastic or ecclesiastical. Sceptical of religious truth, or opposed to religious education.

After the industrial revolution, and especially towards the end of the nineteenth century, there were considerable changes and great material improvements in society. This earthly life, this secular existence, became, for some people, the only thing of importance. It was tangible. It could be seen. It could be measured. Hence the rationalists and secularists were close allies. The third group were the humanists.

> HUMANISM – Devotion to the human interest. System of thought or action concerned with merely human interest (as distinct from divine).

To the humanists, only their fellow human beings and future generations of human beings were of importance. To them it was necessary to improve society morally and economically so that a better quality of life could be enjoyed by all. Thus these humanists had strong links with the secularists and the rationalists. In fact it is impossible to draw clear, distinct lines around these three groups. They had much in common; and their differences, to an outsider, appear only minor.

The Challenge of Charles Bradlaugh

One of the most colourful characters of the nineteenth century was the rationalist and secularist, Charles Bradlaugh. He was a boisterous man of boundless energy and full of good cheer. In 1866 he founded the National Secular Society, the first society of its type. In one year alone he addressed over 276 secularist meetings – and remember how difficult travel was over a hundred years ago.

Bradlaugh loved to be sensational, and enjoyed shocking the establishment. One of his meetings, for example, was advertised as follows:

The Bible: What Is It?

Being an examination thereof from Genesis to Revelation, intended to relieve the Society for Promoting Christian Knowledge from the labour of retranslating the Bible, by proving that it is not worth the trouble and expense.

It would have been interesting to have been present at that meeting, or to have a script of that address. We can only wonder what Bradlaugh said, and speculate whether or not all his colleagues agreed with his claim that 'it is not worth the trouble and expense'.

One such colleague was another secularist named John Stuart Mill, a very intelligent man and one of the broadest minded figures of that era. He was undoubtedly a great supporter of the humanist view concerning the improvability of man. This view claims that when people's material circumstances improve, then people improve as human beings. When they have enough to eat and drink, and can provide themselves with clothes and a house, then crime and moral offences will decrease. We, in today's society, have seen that this view is quite mistaken, but in the nineteenth century the evidence to disprove it was lacking.

John Stuart Mill saw education as one of the ways of improving man. An educated man was more likely to obtain a job, which would not only be more suitable for him, but also provide a higher salary and thus a better life. Mill wrote to his father saying:

I feel as if all would be gained if the whole population were taught to read.

But to read what? Sadly Mill does not elaborate, but reading rubbish will not improve anyone. As Dickens wrote, some years before Mill:

There are books of which the backs and covers are by far the best part.

So what reading matter did Mill have in mind? If he shared the views of Bradlaugh, then he would think that the Bible was 'not worth the trouble and expense'. But if the aim and desire was to improve the lot, material and moral, of the whole population, then what book has done more than the Bible for moulding a moralistic and better society?

Since the production of the King James Authorized Version in 1611, the Bible in English has been readily available, and has had a significant effect upon many human lives. If Mill and Bradlaugh had taken just a glance into what was, for them, recent history, they would have seen the tremendous benefits society had gained from people inspired by the Bible. For example:

William Wilberforce 1759-1833
Christian
English Member of Parliament: 1780-1825
Devoted himself to the cause of the abolition of the slave trade and slavery

Elizabeth Fry 1780-1845
Christian
Reformer
Celebrated for her efforts to improve the state of English prisons and of convicts on their voyage to Australia

Lord Shaftesbury 1801-1885
Christian
Member-of Parliament: 1826-1851
Leading spirit in the movement for reform of working conditions in factories
Philanthropist
Active in many movements for the protection of working classes and the benefit of the poor.

And if Bradlaugh had just taken a look over his shoulder, he would have seen two people who were very inspired by the teachings of the Bible. They were starting something very significant. These were:

William and Catherine Booth (1829-1912 & 1829-1890)
1865 The East London Christian Mission
1878 The Salvation Army
And the Salvation Army is now second only to the government in the provision of social services to the needy in Britain.

And there have been many, many other examples; to name but three which started in the 20th century:

Oxfam

Oxfam was originally founded in Oxford in 1942 as the **Ox**ford Committee for **Fam**ine Relief by a group of Quakers, social activists, and Oxford academics. The original committee included Canon Theodore Richard Milford, and met in the Old Library of University Church of St. Mary the Virgin, not far from the Quaker Meeting House.

Christian Aid

Christian Aid was originally known as Christian Reconstruction in Europe. It was initially concerned with issues of post-World War II welfare, and helped to resettle refugees. It became part of the British Council of Churches (now Churches Together in Britain and Ireland) in 1949, and changed its name to Christian Aid in 1964.

Tear Fund

Tear Fund was created out of the Evangelical Alliance and the Evangelical Refugee Fund created by the United Nations. Its original name was The Evangelical Alliance Relief Fund Committee. It was registered as a charity in 1973, and its leading supporter has been Sir Cliff Richard.

The 21st century has opened with a barrage of aggressive atheism, where people like Richard Dawkins have stated that little or no good comes out of religion. However, one wonders where society would be today without the four organizations mentioned on the previous page, and there are many more, the founders of which have been inspired by what they have read in the Bible. Two of the most recent ones, started in the 21st century, are **Christians Against Poverty**, who help and advise people in serious debt, and the **Street Pastors** initiative, which does wonders on Friday and Saturday nights, saving young people from themselves, each other and the police.

One may share Mill's view about the importance of reading but reading alone will not solve society's problems; it depends upon what is read. It is interesting to note that the importance placed upon reading and writing, which arose in the latter half of the 19th century, is still alive today – and rightly so. On the side of the United States' 1 cent stamp we read:

The ability to write – **a** root of democracy.

With the ability to write goes the related ability to read. However, in studying the literature of the 19th century one had the feeling that people like Mill would have said:

The ability to write – **THE** root of democracy.

The Americans, however, have not made that mistake. The ability to write, and read, is not THE root. It is one of the roots, and another is *what you read* ... but there are others also!

So far we have *hinted* that the Bible should be read; but as George says in *Jumpers* "the onus of proof has passed from the atheist to the believer." Therefore we must proceed to show that the Bible is a peculiar book, in the sense that it is *unique, special* and *extraordinary* – and that it is well worth reading.

Samuel Butler said, "Books should be tried by a judge and jury, as though they were crimes, and counsel should be heard on both sides."

"The noes have it now," says George. "So we, the 'ayes', the believers, must present our case!"

The Case for Reading the Bible

In *Jumpers* George goes on to say:

A small number of men, by the exercise of their intellects, and by the study of the works both of nature and of other intellects before them, have been able to argue coherently against the existence of God. A much larger number of men, by exercise of their emotional and psychological states, have affirmed that this is the correct view. This view derives partly from what is known as common sense, whose virtue, uniquely amongst virtues, is that everybody has it; and partly from the mounting implausibility of a technological age as having divine origins – for while a man might believe that the providence of sheep's wool was made in heaven, he finds it harder to believe the same for Terylene mixture or nylon tights.

We could modify the above and replace 'the existence of God' with 'the authority of the Bible' or even, bearing in mind Bradlaugh's view, 'the reading of the Bible'.

Now, considering the great desire of the rationalists, secularists and humanists to improve the lot of their fellow men, it seems strange that they did not consider the Bible to be of any use. Didn't they realize that between its covers lay a wealth of inspirational material? They had only to see the effect it had upon the lives of William Wilberforce, Elizabeth Fry, Lord Shaftesbury, and William and Catherine Booth, and to note the dramatic effect these five alone had upon society.

Another leading figure of that era, and one from which society benefited greatly, was W.E. Gladstone, four times prime minister. In his famous speech in Liverpool on 28 June 1886 he stated:

All the world over,
I will back the masses
against the classes.

Gladstone introduced voting by ballot. He was a profoundly religious man and a great classical scholar. To him the Bible was 'the impregnable rock of Holy Scripture'.

We mentioned earlier:

- the work of Wilberforce in abolishing slavery,
- the work of Fry in reforming prisons,
- the work of Shaftesbury in reforming conditions in factories, so necessary once the Industrial Revolution was under way,
- the work of William and Catherine Booth, in caring for the poor, uneducated, deprived,
- the work of OXFAM, Christian Aid, Tear Fund, and
- the work of Christians Against Poverty and the Street Pastors.

What did people such as these and Gladstone learn from the Bible? What is there of value, from the sociological point of view, in the Bible? As well as answering these questions, we shall also draw attention to other valuable points which demonstrate why every thinking person, with a concern for society, can learn much from reading and studying the Bible.

Points to be Considered

Point 1 – The time and the Society

The first five books of the Old Testament are Genesis, Exodus, Leviticus, Numbers and Deuteronomy – often known as '*the books of the Law*'; as *the Torah*, the Hebrew for 'teaching'; and as *the Pentateuch*, from the Greek *penta* meaning five and *teuch* meaning book. They are generally accepted as being the oldest writings of the Old Testament – although a case can be made for the book of Job being one of the earliest. Most of the Pentateuch was written by Moses, who lived about 1571 to 1451 BC (*The Companion Bible*, at Appendix 50).

Most of the books of the New Testament were written in the second half of the first century AD, i.e. before AD 100, and probably before AD 70 as *no* New Testament document mentions the fall of Jerusalem to the Romans which took place that year. Thus we can see that the writers of the Bible span nearly 1,600 years. What a great variety of times, places, peoples and societies they must have experienced! All in all, they covered a period of about sixty specific generations. What changes there must have been! But we are talking about the writers themselves. The events described by those writers span a time, not of 1,600 years, but of 4,000 years or so. In the Bible we have some of the world's earliest recorded events.

Some people question the validity of events prior to Moses' day, but we leave any comment upon this to the next chapters. However if we go from Moses' time onwards, what do we have?

A society which is under slavery, in the grip of the powerful Egyptian nation.
A society which escapes to freedom, but which spends forty years wandering and struggling in the wilderness.
A society which, under the military generalship of Joshua, enters and conquers a land.
A society which lives in that land under the rule of judges.
A society which wants a change; they want a king and desire to be a kingdom.
A society which, under King David, goes to war and expands.
A society which, under King Solomon, is prosperous and at peace but ... decadence sets in.
A society which, after Solomon's reign, suffers civil war and is split in two.
A society which is conquered, and comes under the domination of the autocratic King Nebuchadnezzar of Babylon.
A society which is taken by that king into exile to the land of Babylon.
A society which sees the Medo-Persians conquer the Babylonian Empire.
A society which is allowed, by the benign King of Persia, to return to its homeland.
A society which, in its homeland, sees Greece conquer the Medo-Persian Empire and rule.
A society which sees Rome conquer Greece and impose severe rule.

Almost slaves again under Roman rule! Who could set them free this time?

Now, as we look around the world at this present time, what do we see?

- Some nations in the powerful grip of others.
- Some nations attacking others.

- Some nations trying to come to grips with an increase in their wealth, and the power that it brings.
- Some nations trying to come to grips with the problems of prosperity, and the permissiveness that it brings.
- Some nations...

We could go on and draw more parallels, but sufficient has been said to show that the Bible does contain a great deal which is of value to us who live in this century and society.

Point 2 – The place and the environment

Geography can be very important in the development of a society, and the immediate environment can have a great effect upon the people. Britain's particular differences from her European Union partners are due, in part, to her being an island. As well as being influenced by this, the attitude of each individual is also determined by what one experiences in life. By considering the location of a writer we can learn much. First the personal circumstances of some of the writers of the Bible:

While writing, David was at war,
       but Solomon wrote during a 40-year reign of peace.
While writing, Moses was free and wandering in
       a wilderness, but Jeremiah wrote from a dungeon.
  While writing, Luke was free and travelling,
       but John was confined to the Isle of Patmos,
       when writing Revelation.
Daniel wrote some of his prophecies from a palace,
       and some from a hillside.
Paul wrote some of his epistles from friends' houses while free,
       but others he wrote from a Roman prison.

Again we can see what a wealth of learning there is for the one who wishes to take advantage of it, but there is more. Those personal circumstances took place in a variety of countries. In fact the Bible was written in three continents:

Asia ... Africa ... Europe,

Moses wrote while traveling from Egypt to the borders of the land of Canaan, having been freed from the Egyptians.

Jeremiah was in a dungeon in Jerusalem, when the Jewish nation was threatened by the Babylonian Empire.

Daniel wrote from a palace and a hillside in Babylon and Persia, when those powers were dominant.

Luke wrote while travelling around the cities of the Mediterranean, which were all under the Roman Empire.

Paul wrote from homes in Corinth and Philippi, cities under Roman rule. He also wrote when he was in prison in Rome, when Rome ruled the world, including the Jewish nation.

We need only add that some parts of the Bible were written from the heights of happiness and joy while others were written from the depths of despair and sorrow. Surely no other book contains so much information which is as valuable in helping mankind lead a full and contented life.

Finally we should point out that the Bible was written in three languages. The bulk of the Old Testament was written in Hebrew but parts were written in a language called Chaldee or Aramaic. The whole of the New Testament was written in Greek, which was the international language of the first century AD. Whether a culture affects a language, or vice versa, is not the subject of this book. Whichever it may be, we have so much material here which is of immense value to the thinking reader of the Bible.

Point 3 – The writers ... and their writing

Having considered when the writers wrote, the type of society they lived in and its geography, whether near or far, we should now take a look at the writers themselves. In most societies, until recently, writing was the prerogative of the privileged few, those who could afford to learn to write or afford to pay a scribe to do it. Do we find this to be the case with the writers of the Bible? When we look at the Bible we find that amongst those who wrote were:

kings and courtiers
soldiers and shepherds
legislators and statesmen
herdsmen and fishermen
prophets and priests
a despised tax gatherer
a Gentile doctor
a tent-making rabbi.

Let us look again at some of the individual writers and compare and contrast them as people:

David, the writer of many of the 150 psalms in the book of Psalms, rose from the position of a shepherd boy to become King of Israel, to expand the nation through war and to live in a palace.

Solomon, his son, wrote many of the proverbs in the Book of Proverbs. He was raised in that palace as a prince. Throughout his reign there was peace and prosperity. The nation was at its most influential.

Nebuchadnezzar contributed part of the book of Daniel. He was a great Gentile king who conquered the land of Israel, ruled the then known world, and Jews in exile to Babylon.

In contrast to these we have:

Nehemiah, who wrote the book of Nehemiah, was a cup bearer who helped rebuild the walls and gates of Jerusalem when the Jews returned from the Babylonian exile.

Again:

Daniel, who wrote most of the book of Daniel, was one of the bright young men of Jerusalem whom Nebuchadnezzar took to Babylon to educate. He rose to be third in that kingdom.

Paul, who wrote most of the letters in the New Testament, was another highly educated man from the university town of Tarsus, but was one who could use his hands; he was a tentmaker.

In contrast to these we have:

Nehemiah, who wrote the book of Nehemiah, was a cupbearer who helped rebuild the walls and gates of Jerusalem when the Jews returned from the Babylonian exile.

Again:

Daniel, who wrote most of the book of Daniel, was one of the bright young men of Jerusalem whom Nebuchadnezzar took to Babylon to educate. He rose to be third in that kingdom.

Paul, who wrote most of the letters in the New Testament, was another highly educated man from the university town of Tarsus, but was one who could use his hands; he was a tentmaker.

In contrast to these we have:

Peter – a simple fisherman; wrote two New Testament letters.
Amos – an uneducated herdsman; wrote of the book of Amos.

We could compare and contrast many more:

Luke – a highly trained and respected Gentile doctor, wrote the gospel of Luke, and the Acts of the Apostles.
Matthew–a despised tax gatherer; wrote the gospel of Matthew.

Point 4 – The style of the writings

But *what* did these people, these kings and peasants, philosophers and fishermen, statesmen and scholars, write about? We shall not be concerned with the exact content at the moment but will look at the style. There is a book called *The Bible, Designed to be Read as Literature.* The title is suggestive. What types of literature are there in the Bible? We have already mentioned that some wrote from heights of happiness, while others wrote from depths of despair. Thus we expect variety, but when we look at it, the variety is staggering. The Bible contains:

Love and drama
History and biography
Allegory and figurative writings
       Personal correspondence
       Personal memoirs
       Diaries
Religious poetry
Lyrical poetry
Songs
       Parables
       Proverbs
       Philosophy
Prophetic utterances
Apocalyptic revelation
Formal, instructional writings.

As well as all these, there is also *the Law*. And what law it is! There is:

  Civil law and Criminal law and Ethical law
      Religious law and Ritual Law
        Dietary law and Sanitary law

Is anything not covered?

Collecting Thoughts

With so many types of people writing in widely varying circumstances at so many different times and producing such a diversity, we might think that the Bible is a mere anthology, or collection of writings; but, as F.F. Bruce says, in *The Book and the Parchments:*

> The Bible is not simply an anthology; there is a unity which binds the whole together. An anthology is compiled by an anthologist, *but no anthologist compiled the Bible.*

The writers of the Bible commented upon dozens of different subjects, many of them controversial; but throughout the whole book there is an unfolding of one particular theme, namely God's redemption of man. This is shown in the titles of certain books written about the Bible, such as *The unfolding Drama of Redemption* by Graham Scroggie, or *The Unfolding Purpose of God* by Stuart Allen.

This theme runs throughout the whole book from Genesis to Revelation. It binds the whole together, and although many other subjects are covered, to miss the vital plan of redemption, salvation and atonement, is like omitting the blood system from an analysis of the human body. The blood system is essential for the life of the body. The plan of redemption is essential for the life of the Bible, which is eternal life.

A Peculiar Book
and Well-Worth Reading

Some readers may think that the word *peculiar* is inappropriate to describe the Bible, but the word has two meanings:

PECULIAR – (1) Strange, odd.
                    (2) Special, extraordinary.

In today's society most people think that the Bible is a peculiar book, in the sense of the former meaning of that word. To them it is strange and odd. We hope that our readers, who have followed our arguments, will also say that the Bible is a peculiar book, but we hope that they mean special, extraordinary! Having just considered:

the time and the society,
the place and the environment,
the writers and the writing,

I hope most minds would declare that the Bible is very special, very extraordinary. Some may even go further and declare that, among books, it is UNIQUE.

UNIQUE – Of which there is only one.
Unmatched and unequalled.
Having no like or equal.
Different from all others.
The one and only.

Surely there is no book like it. There is only one Bible. It is unmatched and unequalled. It is different from all other books. It is the one and only! Yes, it is unique and, as such, surely it deserves to be read by everyone. We can learn much from it on a great variety of subjects. If our aim is the improvement of our society, then the Bible is a must! And yet ... so many find the Bible difficult, and almost impossible to read. Why is this? To quote Professor Bruce again:

Any part of the human body can only be properly explained in reference to the whole body. And any part of the Bible can only be explained in reference to the whole Bible.

The Bible is a big book, and understanding it is made much easier if the gist of that *unfolding Drama of Redemption* and the main points of that *Unfolding Purpose of God* are known. For that reason, together with my wife, we wrote *Introducing God's Plan* – also published by the Open Bible Trust – which covers the main thrust of the Bible, in sixteen easy to read chapters.

However, before moving on we now give the outline of the Plan of God as revealed in the Bible. Once having seen the outline, the reader will then be able to slot in the detail of the Bible in the appropriate places.

The Outline of the Plan

The first book of the Bible opens with an account of the creation, yet only a few short pages are devoted to this mighty event. It is quickly passed over because the creation of this world is insignificant when compared with the purpose for which it was intended. Thus although we would dearly love to know more about *how* it was created, we are told much, much more about *why* it was created.

It was created to be inhabited by men and women; and these were a special creation of God, made in the likeness of his image, created good, but ... with the ability to choose. They were not puppets or robots. God already had a mechanical creation in the sun, the moon and stars; these (*almost*) always obeyed the prescribed laws. But not ... here, with the man and the woman, was the ability to respond, to love, to obey ... to disobey! Sadly the record shows wrong choices, disobedience, and thus sin (which means 'to come short') entered into the lives of the man and woman, to be followed later by death.

From that small, almost insignificant first act of disobedience, things grew much worse. Instead of deciding to eat of a prohibited fruit, as his parents had done, Cain murdered his brother. Things deteriorated rapidly, and by Noah's time the extreme sinfulness and violence of mankind grieved God. It was so bad that humanity, excluding Noah and his family, were destroyed by the Flood. However, afterwards God gave his first covenant to mankind, namely that the world would never again be destroyed by water. But did mankind learn its lesson?

The building of the Tower at Babel was another wrong choice, a sign of open rebellion against God; and it led to mankind being dispersed over the world. But who was to teach these nations about God and his ways? Abraham was selected by God, and God promised him that he was to be the father of a great nation, the Jewish nation; and that they were to become a kingdom of priests, and take the teaching of God to the whole world. God was to provide them with a land; but first, they were to be slaves in Egypt. ("God moves in a mysterious way his wonders to perform", the title of a hymn by William Cowper.)

After 215 years in Egypt, the leader Moses arose; and the book of Exodus is an account of the Jewish nation's escape from Egypt, and their journey in the wilderness. There, through Moses, God gave the nation the Law contained in Leviticus and Deuteronomy, and taught the people through the priests. There they learnt that death was the result of sin, and that sin could be forgiven only through a sacrifice that was yet to come.

After forty years in the wilderness, the Jews entered the land which had been promised to them by God. Joshua was their leader, and they settled in that land, and the Law was administered by the Judges. Eventually, however, the people desired a king, and Saul was the first king, followed by David and then Solomon. But calamity! At the end of Solomon's reign, civil war broke out, and the Jewish nation split in two. The division produced two kings and two priesthoods, and often both were corrupt. These two nations, Israel and Judah, turned from God. So the prophets were sent by God to the people and their rulers, with warnings that if they did not repent and turn back to God, there would be judgment.

Judgment came; first one part of the divided nation (Israel) was exiled to Assyria, and then the other part (Judah) was taken to Babylon. Eventually Medo-Persia took over the Babylonian Empire, and let a remnant of the Jews return to Jerusalem and the surrounding land. There the Jews rebuilt the city and the temple. There they waited, next under the domination of first the Greeks and then the Romans, until the birth of the Messiah.

But the Prophets had been given two pictures of the Messiah: the Messiah-ben-David, the glorious, powerful king; and, the Messiah-ben-Joseph, the lowly, suffering one. Under the domination of Rome, the Jews looked for the glorious, powerful king. Christ Jesus, the lowly and meek one, with his teaching of love and forgiveness, was not for them. They crucified him. But the grave could not hold the 'Prince of Peace' (Isaiah 9:6). He broke the bonds of death and rose triumphantly from the dead, and his resurrection is a permanent testimony to there being life after death. After such an outstanding event he ascended into heaven to the glory which he had had with God before he entered this world as a babe in Bethlehem.

His death and resurrection is the focal point of the Bible. It made possible the fulfilment of God's purpose for mankind. Christ died as the sin offering for the world, the sin sacrifice the Jewish people had been taught about in the Law. His sacrifice enabled Peter, on the day of Pentecost, to call on the Jewish people to repent of their sins, and especially of their sin of crucifying Christ. On that day Peter had been baptized in the Holy Spirit, and he was full of the Spirit when he spoke. The initial response amongst the Jews was great, but as time went on their hearts hardened. The first Gentiles, (i.e. non-Jews, people from other nations), were later given the message and gladly received the promise of eternal life and the forgiveness of sin through believing in Christ's sin offering on the cross. These Gentiles received this gospel of salvation more eagerly than the majority of the Jews, who were becoming hostile.

About thirty-five years after Christ's death, resurrection and ascension, James the brother of Christ, and leader of the church in Jerusalem, was stoned to death on orders of Ananus the high priest (see Josephus, *Antiquities of the Jews* 20, 9, 1). At about the same time, Paul met the Jewish leaders in Rome, and disagreement amongst them resulted in the Jewish nation being set aside by God (Acts 28:25-28). Shortly afterwards, in AD 70, Jerusalem was sacked by the Romans, the temple was destroyed, and the Jews were largely dispersed from their land by the Romans, who scattered them throughout the Roman Empire.

The great and glorious message concerning the salvation of God was then sent directly to Gentiles, and the Christian message spread throughout the Roman world. This gospel of salvation by grace through faith in the Lord Jesus Christ's death and resurrection has now been preached throughout most of the world. But what about God's initial promises to Abraham and to the Jewish nation? How will these be fulfilled?

These events still lie in the future, and are the subject of the prophetic parts of the Bible. These prophecies show that the Jewish nation is to be re-gathered to Jerusalem and the surrounding land, and that Christ is to come again to them – this time as the glorious, powerful king. Under his rule they will go out to all the people of the world and teach them about God and his plan for salvation, including the forgiveness of sins and eternal life. Then will follow a glorious time of peace on earth which is to last for 1,000 years, but which is to be ended by one final act of rebellion against God. This he instantly and completely destroys, and afterwards creates a new heaven and a new earth 'the home of righteousness'. Righteousness is to be the character of this new creation. There is to be no more sorrow and no more tears. There will be no more sin and no more death. The former things will have passed away, and this creation will be populated by those people to whom God has granted eternal life. Perfection will have been achieved. God will be all in all.

Final Questions

Does anyone still think the Bible not worth reading? Does anyone still think there is nothing we can learn from it? Does anyone still side with Charles Bradlaugh, and say that such a book is not worth the trouble and expense of translation into one's own language? The answer must surely be – **there is no one.**

Section 2:
The Bible!
A Reliable Book?
Is It Worth Studying?

Many books require no thought from those who read them, and for a very simple reason – they made no such demand upon those who wrote them!

(CHARLES CALEB COLTON, 1780 – 1832)

Please return this book; I find that though many of my friends are poor arithmeticians, they are nearly all good book-keepers.

(SIR WALTER SCOTT, 1771-1832)

And further, by these, my son, be admonished; of making many books there is no end; and much study is a weariness of the flesh.

(ECCLESIASTES 12:12 KJV)

Never lend books, for no one returns them; the only books I have in my library are books other people have lent me.

(ANATOLE FRANCE, 1844-1924)

The Bible:
To be Read ... Yes! But Study?

"There are books of which the backs and covers are by far the best parts," said Charles Dickens. Such books are not even worth reading, and it would appear that many books fall into this category: Charles Caleb Colton had written earlier: "Many books require no thought from those who read them, and for a very simple reason – they made no such demand upon those who wrote them!"

A book that requires little thought may be just the thing to read last thing at night or when one is recovering from an illness or accident. Such light material has a place, but one would never study it, simply because one couldn't study it! There is nothing in it to study.

If a book is worth studying then there must be something special about it. If such a book is dealing with fiction, then what that special something is may be difficult to define and there may be grounds for disagreement. In most other areas, however, the reliability of the information contained in a book is one necessary, special item. Geography books which did not accurately record the details of a country would not only misinform a student, but would totally mislead a visitor. The accuracy of road maps affects most people nowadays, and with new roads opening all the time, one has to buy a new road atlas every other year. Similarly a diarist, who does not impartially and accurately record the information of his days, detracts greatly from the value of his writings. For a history book to be of value it must be reliable, it needs to be accurate – and here we have an interesting subject.

There is a tremendous difference between history books and historical novels. The former attempt to discover the facts, whereas the latter take certain of the facts and weave a thread of fiction through them. Such weaving may be slight, but it could equally be so extensive that the facts are submerged under a mound of fiction.

The Lion in Winter by James Goldman is well worth reading or watching on stage or screen, but is it worth studying? As fictional literature the answer may well be 'yes'; but as history, the answer is more likely to be 'no'. *Myself as Witness* Goldman's next book, concerns itself with the times of King John and the Magna Carta the following is quoted from James Goldman's introductory 'Note to the reader' (italics are ours):

> I have put my Chronicle in the hands of Giraldus Cambrensis, as distinguished an author as there was in England at this time. He knew John and his family intimately; he was much involved with the Plantagenets. But in the years the novel covers, he *was not among those present*. He was living in retirement in Lincoln ... I have written what he *might* have told us.

Thus in Goldman's historical novel the main observer, a person who actually lived at the time but who never saw any of the action described, is moved from Lincoln to London. The novel is presented through his eyes, although he was never there! This may be good fiction, but it cannot do anything but confuse historical fact. This is certainly true of the novels and plays, relating to the reign of Queen Elizabeth I. Having seen some of the plays, read some of the historical novels together with some of the history books, one is so confused that one can no longer recall what is fact and what is fiction! Is the Bible like that? Is it a historical novel? A mixture of fact and fiction? Or is it historically reliable?

If it is a type of historical novel, a mixture of fact and fiction, then it may be worthy of study as literature. If it can be shown to be historically reliable, then it will definitely be worth studying, for we have seen, in Chapter 1, the vast scope of the Bible.

Now some may think that to investigate the reliability of the Bible is most inappropriate but... There is no virtue now in blind reliance.

One heartily agrees with that quote from Sydney Keyes' *The Kestrel*, but one could present a case for the deletion of the word 'now'. There never has been, nor ever will be, any virtue in blind reliance. If the Bible is reliable then it must be seen to be reliable. We proceed to put the case.

Points to be Considered

Point 1 – How do we know what happened in the past?

If anything happens in the world today we believe it has happened because we see it on the television, hear about it on the radio or read about it in the papers. Provided there is no censorship of the media, we can be reasonably sure that most of what we see, hear and read is correct. Commentary on the news may be somewhat biased, and there may well be the odd mistake in reporting but, in general, the bulk of what is reported is reliable.

The same is true about the recent past, and to the evidence of video tapes, films, newspaper and magazine libraries we can add that of books which deal with recent events. However, if we go back 100 years ... no television! Go back a little further ... no films or radio! Go back further still ... no newspapers as we know them today and not even 'brown and white' sepia photographs! There are just the books: history books and diaries. Thus when dealing with the events of two hundred or more years ago, we have to rely on the writings of people who were alive at that time and who recorded the events then, or shortly afterwards. Again, their views may have been a little biased one way or another and there may be the odd mistake but, in general, if the writer was attempting to be honest and fair, most of what he recorded would be reliable.

But what about the distant past? The original writings have become decayed, damaged or worn out. Copies may have been made and we have to rely on copies of the original, or copies of copies of the original, or copies of copies of copies ... etc. So with ancient documents, as well as the possibility of bias and error in the original, there is also the possibility of errors creeping in through copying, to say nothing of deliberate additions, deletions and alterations which a biased copyist could introduce. Therefore when we look at the reliability of ancient historical books, four points should be noted:

(1) The date of the original writings.

(2) The date of the earliest copy now available.

(3) The time elapsed between the original writings and the earliest copy.

(4) The number of copies now available.

For example, a writer might have written about:

(1) A battle in the year 150 BC.

(2) The earliest copy now available is dated AD 1100.

(3) The time elapsed was 1,250 years – the difference between 150 BC and AD 1100.

(4) The number of copies is 12.

We can do this for many different ancient books, and thus see which are likely to be the most reliable. Obviously, in general:

- The earlier the date of the earliest copy – the better.
- The shorter the time elapsed between the original writing and the earliest copy – the better.
- The greater the number of copies – the better.

As a real example, compare the works of Herodotus, the ancient Greek historian, and Aristophanes, the playwright from ancient Athens. Which is likely to be the more reliable? The facts are as follows:

Herodotus	Aristophanes
Written between 485 -425 BC	Written between 448-385 BC
Earliest copy, AD 900.	Earliest copy, AD 900.
Years elapsed, between 1325-1365.	Years elapsed, between 1285-1348.
Number of copies, 8.	Number of copies, 10.

With the writings of these two, it is a close thing, Aristophanes may just get the vote as there are two more manuscripts and the earliest copy is forty years closer to the date of the original.

Let us compare two others: the writings of Plato, the classical Greek philosopher and mathematician, and Sophocles, the ancient Greek playwright.

Plato	Sophocles
Written between 428-348 BC	Written between 496-405 BC
Earliest copy, AD 900.	Earliest copy, AD 1000.
Years elapsed, 1248-1328	Years elapsed, 1405-1496
Number of copies, 7.	Number of copies, 100.

Which is likely to be the more reliable? Although the time elapsed for the copies of Plato's writings is some 150 years less than for those of Sophocles, there are only seven copies compared to a hundred copies of the writings of Sophocles. We can see that we are in a difficult area and it would take an expert to decide the issue.

Now compare the following six and see if it is possible to give a clear verdict. Which is likely to be the most reliable?

	A	B	C
Written	AD 75-160	AD 62-113	AD 100
Earliest copy	AD 950	AD 850	AD 1100
Years elapsed	790-875	737-788	1,000
Number of copies	8	7	20
	D	E	F
Written	AD 50-100	59 BC- AD 17	58-50 BC
Earliest copy	AD 350	AD 350	AD 850
Years elapsed	250-300	333-409	900-908
Number of copies	5,000	20	10

Again it is difficult to distinguish between A and B. We may rate them about equal. We would probably rate E more reliable than C. But there can be no doubt about the fact that D stands head and shoulders above the others. There are 5,000 copies with the earliest dating back to only 250 years after the original manuscript. D is undoubtedly the best, the most reliable.

What are A, B, C, D, E, and F? Are they just made up examples? No, they are the actual writings of:

A - The Roman historian Suetonius (*De Vita Caesarum*)
B - The Roman lawyer, magistrate and writer Pliny the Younger (*History*)
C - The Roman senator and historian Tacitus (*Annals*)
D - The New Testament Writers
E - The Roman historian Livy (*Roman History*)
F - Julius Caesar (*Gallic War*)

Yes! The New Testament stands head and shoulders above all the others. To quote F. F. Bruce again (*The New Testament Documents*):

There are in existence about 5,000 Greek manuscripts of the New Testament in whole or in part. The best and most important of these go back to somewhere about AD 350, the two most important being the Codex Vaticanus, the chief treasure of the Vatican Library in Rome, and the well-known Codex Sinaiticus, which the British Government purchased from the Soviet Government for £100,000 on Christmas Day 1933, and which is the chief treasure of the British Museum.

Perhaps we can better appreciate the vast wealth of New Testament manuscripts if we compare the textual evidence which supports them with that for other ancient writings.

Writings of	When written	Earliest copy	Years elapsed	No. of copies
Suetonius	AD 75-160	AD 950	790-875	8
Pliny the Younger	AD 62-113	AD 850	737-788	7
Tacitus (Annals)	AD 100	AD 1100	1,000	20
Tacitus (Minor Works)	AD 100	AD 1100	1,000	1
New Testament	**AD 50-100**	**AD 350**	**250-300**	**5,000**
Livy	59 BC- AD 17	AD 350	333-409	20
Caesar	58-50 BC	AD 850	900-908	10
Catullus	84-54 BC	AD 1550	1,604-1,634	3
Demosthenes	383-322 BC	AD 1100	1,422-1,483	200
Aristotle	384-322 BC	AD 1100	1,422-1,484	5
Plato	427-347 BC	AD 900	1,247-1,327	7
Aristophanes	450-385 BC	AD 900	1,285-1,350	10
Thucydides	460-400 BC	AD 900	1,300-1,360	8
Euripides	480-406 BC	AD 1100	1,506-1,580	9
Sophocles	496-406 BC	AD 1000	1,406-1,496	100
Herodotus	480-425 BC	AD 900	1,325-1,380	8

No matter how we look at it, the New Testament writings come out best. No matter how we arrange the list, the New Testament writings come out on top.

Number of copies
The New Testament	5,000
Demosthenes	200
Sophocles	100
Tactitus and Livy	20

Years elapsed – from the original writing to the earliest copy now available

The New Testament	250-300
Livy	333-409
Pliny	737-788
Suetonius	790-875

But have we been generous to the writings of the New Testament? No! We have purposely selected conservative figures. We could have followed such views as that of A.T. Robertson in *An Introduction to Textual Criticism of the New Testament:*

> There are some 8,000 manuscripts of the Latin Vulgate and at least 1,000 for other earlier editions. Add over 4,000 Greek manuscripts and we have 13,000 manuscripts of portions of the New Testament.

And that figure of 4,000 has, thanks to archaeological discoveries since Robertson wrote his book, risen to 5,000. It is those 5,000 Greek manuscripts only that have been included in the figures given above.

Again, with respect to dating, F.F. Bruce says, in *The New Testament Documents* (italics are ours):

> Earlier still is a fragment of a papyrus codex containing John 18:31-33, 37f, now in the John Rylands Library, Manchester, dated on palaeographical grounds around AD 130, showing that the latest of the four gospels, which was written, according to tradition, at Ephesus between AD 90 and 100, was circulating within forty years of its composition ... It must be regarded as being by half a century, the earliest extant fragment of the New Testament.

Thus the time elapsed for this portion is less than fifty years and, from the last sentence quoted, there are others which date back to within a hundred years of the original writings. Bruce goes on:

No classical scholar would listen to an argument that the authority of Herodotus or Thucydides is in doubt because the earliest manuscripts of their works which are of any use to us are over 1,300 years later than the originals.

How true! No classical scholar would doubt the authenticity of the writings of these two, yet there were just eight *copies* of the originals in each case. How different is the situation of the New Testament scholar who has to defend 5,000 copies of the originals, the earliest written *not* 1,300 years after the events, but a mere 250-300 years! Sadly, that defence has had to be presented not only to hostile atheists but also to the higher critics and modernists within the Christian Church. It is just as well that such people never took up the classics for they would have wiped out many valuable works such as those of Plato! Fortunately the wealth of textual evidence has helped to ensure that the New Testament has survived their onslaughts and is doing well, although no one can deny damage has been done.

J. W. Montgomery writes, in *History and Christianity* (italics are ours):

> To be sceptical of the resultant text of the New Testament is to allow all of classical antiquity to slip into obscurity for *no documents of the ancient period are as well attested bibliographically as the New Testament,*

While in Benjamin Warfield's *Introduction to Textual Criticism of the New Testament, we* read:

> If we compare the present state of the New Testament text with that of any other ancient writing, we must ... declare it to be marvelously correct. Such has been the care with which the New Testament has been copied.

We have said enough to prove the point. No classical scholar, no educationalist, no sociologist would say that, on textual grounds, Plato's Republic is not worth reading, or that the copies are not reliable versions of what was actually written. Similarly, no one can point the finger at the New Testament documents we have available to us today and say that, on textual grounds, they are not reliable versions of those originals which were written in the first century of this era.

But what about the Old Testament?

Point 2 – Are the Old Testament documents reliable?

It is true that the Old Testament does not have the abundance of manuscripts available to support it as does the New Testament. Until fairly recently, the oldest Hebrew copy of the Old Testament was dated around AD 900; and since the Old Testament was completed about 400 BC, the time between the original and the earliest copy available is 1,300 years. Thus at first glance, the reliability of the Old Testament, on textual grounds, would seem no greater than that of the other ancient writings. However two very important factors indicate that this is not the case, and that the Old Testament is far more reliable. These factors are:

1. The Jewish copyist.
2. A recent discovery.

(1) THE JEWISH COPYIST

The Jews regarded their Bible, the Old Testament, as 'the Word of the Lord', and as such they took very great care of the manuscripts. They had an incredibly intricate system for copying the scrolls which contained those Old Testament books.

(1) A synagogue scroll must be written on the skin of a ceremonially clean animal.
(2) These animals and skins must be prepared for the particular use of the synagogue by a Jew.
(3) These skins must be fastened together with strings taken from ceremonially clean animals.
(4) Every skin must contain a certain number of columns of writing, which must be the same throughout the entire copy.

(5) The length of each column of writing must not be less than 48 lines or more than 60 lines, and the breadth of each column must consist of 30 letters.

(6) The whole copy must be first lined; and if three words are written without a line, the copy is considered worthless.

(7) The ink should be black, neither red, green, nor any other colour; and that ink must be prepared according to a definite formula.

(8) The manuscript which is being copied must be an exemplar, i.e. it is considered a perfect manuscript, from which the copyists must not deviate in the least.

(9) No word or letter, not even *a yod* (the smallest letter of the Hebrew alphabet), must be written from memory, the scribe not having looked at the exemplar manuscript before him.

(10) Between every consonant the space of a hair or a thread must intervene.

(11) Between every new section, the breadth of nine consonants must intervene.

(12) Between every book, three lines must intervene.

(13) The fifth book of Moses, Deuteronomy, must end exactly with a complete line of writing; but the rest need not do so.

(14) The copyist must sit in full Jewish dress.

(15) The copyist must, before writing, wash his whole body.

(16) The copyist must not begin to write the name of God with a pen not newly dipped in ink.

(17) Should even a king address the copyist when he is writing the name of God, he must take no notice.

The above is taken from *The Volume of the Book* by C.H. Welch, which quotes from the out of print work by Samuel Davidson called *The Hebrew Text of the Old Testament*. In that book, Davidson went on to say:

> The scrolls in which these regulations are not observed are condemned to be buried in the ground or burned; or they are banished to the schools to be used as reading books.

They could not be used in the synagogue or temple. Scrolls in which these regulations were not observed were not considered authentic – but that is not the end of the story!

Added to all of the above, was the work of the Massorites who were custodians of the Hebrew Old Testament. Their work was not to comment upon the writings, but to preserve them exactly as they had been given. They produced the Massorah. *The Companion Bible* (Appendix 30) tells us that:

> All the oldest and best Manuscripts of the Hebrew Bible contain on every page, besides the Text (which is arranged in two or more columns), a varying number of lines of smaller writings, distributed between the upper and lower margins. This smaller writing is called the *Massorah Magna* or *Great Massorah*, while that in the side margins and between the columns is called the *Massorah Parva* or *Small Massorah*.

The illustration on the next page is most of a reduced facsimile (original size 16 inches x 12 inches) of a manuscript of the Hebrew Bible which is in the British Museum. It shows Daniel 9:17-10:6. In the full manuscript, the Great Massorah is in seven lines of writing in the lower margin and the four lines in the upper margin. In the outer margin and between the three columns is the Small Massorah.

> The *Massorah* is called 'A Fence to the Scriptures', because it locked all words and letters in their places. It does not contain notes or comments as such, but facts and phenomena. It records the number of times that several letters occur in the various books of the Bible; the number of words, and the middle word; the number of verses, and the middle verse; the number of verses, and the middle verse; the number of expressions and combinations of words, etc. All this, not from a perverted ingenuity, but for the set purpose of safeguarding the Sacred Text, *and preventing the loss or misplacement of a single letter or word.*

So why are there so few copies of manuscripts of the Old Testament? When one considers the rules for the copyists and the detailed information of the Massorah for checking each copy, then we can understand why there are relatively few copies, as some would fail the test and be discarded. However, we can also see that the copies which do exist are extremely accurate and reliable. When a copy had passed the tests, the Jews were so convinced that the finished copy was an exact duplicate that they gave this new copy equal authority with the old. The archaeologist Sir Frederic Kenyon tells us (in *Our Bible and the Ancient a Manuscripts*):

The same extreme care which was devoted to the transcriptions is also at the bottom of the disappearance of the earlier copies. When a manuscript had been copied with the exactitude prescribed by the Talmud, and had been duly verified, it was accepted as authentic and regarded as being of equal value with any other copy. If all were equally correct, age gave no advantage to a manuscript; on the contrary, age was a positive disadvantage, since a manuscript was liable to become defaced or damaged in the lapse of time. A damaged or imperfect copy was at once condemned as unfit for use.

So we can see why the Old Testament manuscripts are exceptionally reliable and why, until recently, they were few in number.

(2) AN IMPORTANT DISCOVERY

Until recently, the earliest copies of the Hebrew text of the Old Testament were dated at about AD 900 but the discovery of the Dead Sea Scrolls changed all that. These 'Scrolls' included some 40,000 fragments of writings, and from these over 500 books have been reconstructed. One full scroll, the book of Isaiah, has been dated on palaeographical grounds at 125 BC, just about 500 years after Isaiah lived. Some of the other Old Testament writing among these scrolls have been given earlier dates, up to 200 BC.

> Now, thanks to this very important discovery, we have come to appreciate that the manuscript evidence to support the reliability of the Old Testament is now second only to that which supports the New. The discovery of the Dead Sea Scrolls enabled a very important check to be made on the Jewish copyists. Some critics made much of possible copyists' mistakes in the texts of the Bible; but we have shown that, compared with other ancient writings, there is far more textual support for the New Testament. But what of the Old? It too is freer from error than any other ancient book! Certainly none of the doctrines of the Bible is affected by the few significant alternative readings that there are. Naturally it is impossible to deal with every alternative reading, but we give one example to show how few and how relatively insignificant were the mistakes of the Jewish copyists over a period of 1,000 years.

Before the discovery of the Dead Sea Scrolls, the earliest copy of the book of Isaiah was dated about AD 900, but those scrolls contained a copy dated at 125 BC, a difference of over 1,000 years. Some critics expected to find significant differences between these two scrolls, as during those 1,000 years many copies of copies had been made. As Geisler and Nix point out, in *A General Introduction to the Bible*, if we compare in both scrolls the very famous chapter 53 we find that:

- Of the 166 words of Isaiah 53, there are only seventeen letters in question.
- Ten of these letters are simply a matter of spelling, which does not affect the sense.
- Four more letters are minor stylistic changes, such as conjunctions.
- The remaining three letters comprise the word 'light', which is added in verse 11, and does not affect the meaning greatly.

Thus there are three types of mistake:

1. Spelling mistakes

We can easily appreciate how these would come about in a period of over 1,000 years. We have only to compare changes in spelling in the English language over the last 500 years to realize how such could alter. For example, compare our modern spelling with that of William Tyndale's (1494-1536) version of Genesis 39:2: "And the Lorde was with Ioseph, and he was a luckie felowe."

Considering the criticism made by some about the differences in the various manuscripts of the New Testament, Geisler and Nix comment that:

> There is ambiguity in saying that there are some 20,000 variants in the existing manuscripts of the New Testament ... If one single word is mis-spelled in 3,000 different places, this is counted as 3,000 variants or readings. (See later *Point 3 – How do we get at the original reading?*)

2. Stylistic changes
These involve such words as conjunctions – for example, 'and', 'but', 'yet'. Prepositions are also involved – i.e. words such as 'up', 'in', 'from'. We can easily appreciate how an expression like 'He went into the tent' would turn into 'He went in the tent'. Similarly, 'He rode on his horse' to 'He rode upon his horse'. Again such changes are not likely to affect the sense or meaning of a passage.

3. The addition of a word

With this we should include the omission and alteration of words. This could be serious but, amazingly, it isn't; e.g. the inclusion of the word 'light' in Isaiah 53, as mentioned above. Sir Frederic Kenyon tells us in *Our Bible and the Ancient Manuscripts:*

No fundamental doctrine of the Christian faith rests on a disputed reading.

We give an illustration of an addition or omission – depending on which way you look at it, from 1 Timothy 3:16. The Greek for God is *theos*, but some texts have *os*, which means 'who'. Thus this verse could read either.

> Great is the mystery of godliness: God (*theos*) was manifest in the flesh.

or

> Great is the mystery of godliness: who (*os*) was manifest in the flesh.

Some people have objected greatly to the second possibility, saying that it detracts from the divinity of Christ, but it doesn't. 'Who' is a pronoun and thus must related to a noun. If we look in the near context, the only noun it can relate to is 'God' of verse 15. Thus both readings, are saying exactly the same thing. Sir Frederick Kenyon emphasizes (italics are ours):

> It cannot be too strongly asserted that in substance the text of the Bible is certain! Especially is this the case with the New Testament.[2] The number of manuscripts of the New Testament, of early translations of it, and of quotations from it, is so large that it is practically certain that the true reading of every doubtful passage is preserved in some one or other of the ancient authorities. This can be said of no other ancient book in the world.

Sir Frederic Kenyon was director and principal librarian of the British Museum, and second to none in authority for issuing statements about ancient manuscripts. A statement such as the above, from one of the greatest authorities in the field of New Testament criticism, cannot be ignored. It is a weighty comment, and it raises three further points for discussion.

---

[2] This was written before the discovery of the Dead Sea Scrolls.

(a) If the true reading is contained in one or other of the ancient manuscripts – how do we get at it? How do we get the original?

(b) The testimony of the early translators is mentioned. Is it significant?

(c) The testimony of the early Christian writers is mentioned. Is that significant?

Point 3 – How do we get towards the original reading?

This is not easy to do when dealing with ancient manuscripts, but with the Bible the task is made so much simpler because of the comparative lack of errors. To demonstrate this, we can compare the New Testament with the *Iliad* of Homer, which was also considered sacred, and with the *Mahabharata*, the national epic of India. (The following information is from Geisler and Nix, *A General Introduction to the Bible*; in turn from Bruce Metzger, for the Iliad and Mahabharata data.)

Book	New Testament	Iliad	Mahabharata
Lines in the book	20,000	15,600	250,000
Number of "significant":			
- alternative-reading lines	40	764	26,000
- alternative-readings	~400	~7,640	~260,000
Percentage of "significant"			
- alternative readings.	0.2%	4.9%	10.4%

So, about 99.8 percent of the New Testament is without "significant" alternative readings; and these are spread throughout the text. According to Geisler and Nix, the New Testament text is "pure whether the critic adopts the Textus Receptus [Received Text, RT], Majority Text [MT], Nestle-Aland Text [NA(/UBS3)], or some eclectic text ..."[3]

---

[3] In the main RT and NA Greek texts, the word-counts agree 98.2% at 140,553 and 138,020 words. [Bible numeric UK data; see Index-1 link].

But what about the Old Testament? It is more difficult to judge, but a comparison of the standard Hebrew text used today with that of the Dead Sea Scrolls was made by Gleason Archer *in a Survey of the Old Testament*. He found that they:

> ... proved to be word for word identical ... in more than 95% of the text. The 5% variation consisted chiefly of obvious slips of the pen and variations in spelling.

With such accurate manuscripts to work with, the task of reconstruction of the original is made far easier. Say, for example, we have eleven manuscripts labeled A1, B1, C1, D1, E1, F1, G1, H1, I1, J1 and K1. By close scrutiny and comparison, it is possible to group them together in twos or threes or fours (or more) and to construct the manuscript from which they were copied. For example:

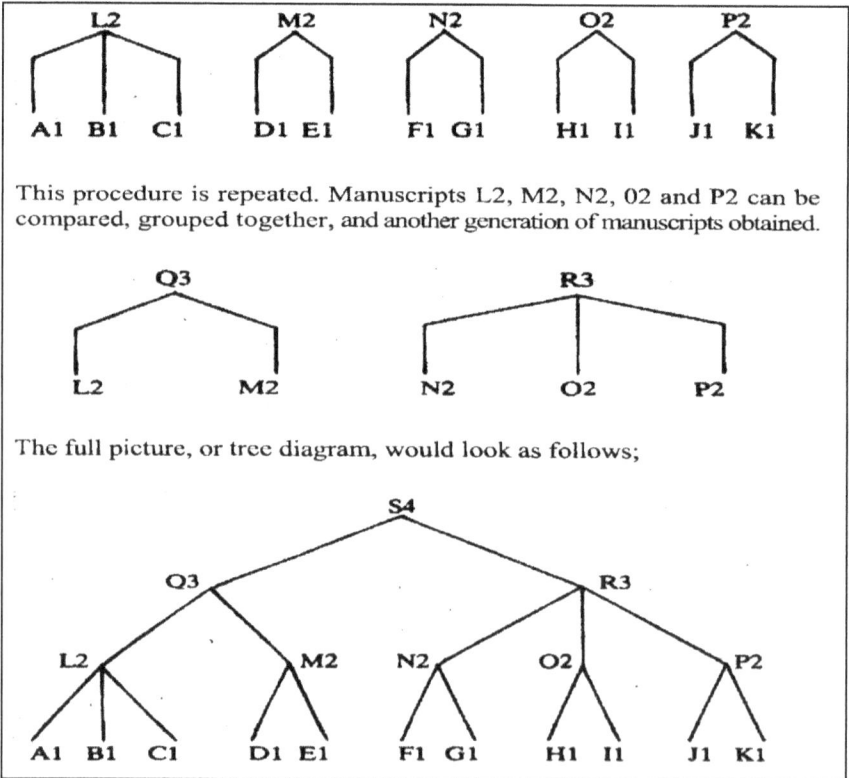

This procedure is repeated. Manuscripts L2, M2, N2, 02 and P2 can be compared, grouped together, and another generation of manuscripts obtained.

The full picture, or tree diagram, would look as follows;

Thus starting off with the manuscripts A1, B1, C1 ... K1, it is possible to construct the manuscript, S4, which will be practically identical with the original. Naturally the above is an over-simplification of a very specialized procedure, but it demonstrates clearly what has to be done.

Point 4 – The testimony of the early translators; is it significant?

The first major translation of the Old Testament was into Greek and took place in the third century BC. Traditionally it is said to have been made by 72 Palestinian Jews in just 72 days and thus it is called the Septuagint (abbreviated to LXX), from the Latin Septuaginta, meaning seventy.

However, as a testimony to the reliability of the Bible we turn to the translations made in the early centuries of this AD era. The earliest were translated into Syriac (closely related to Aramaic), Latin and Coptic (Egyptian), as well as into the languages of Armenia and Georgia. Those translations, when compared to the Greek manuscripts we now have, also show almost insignificant variation. Charles H. Welch, in his book "True from the Beginning," writes:

> Before the close of the second century, translations of the NT began to be made, and this effectively prevented any alterations, additions or subtractions, for such a fraud would immediately become known and exposed – unless, indeed, we are credulous enough to believe that friends and foes, of different nations, languages and opinions, shall all without exception have agreed to countenance such a fraud.

> In the third edition of the Encyclopedia Britannica we read: "This argument is so strong, that, if we deny the authenticity of the NT, we may with a thousand times greater propriety reject all the other writings in the world."

That last sentence is, indeed, strong!

Point 5 – The testimony of the early Christian writers; is it significant?

We can see that the rules for the Jewish copyist of the Old Testament and the very great number and very early date of the New Testament manuscripts, have ensured that errors of any description have been kept to a minimum. The early translations have also enabled us to see that the alternative readings were not deliberately introduced. To this testimony must be added that of the early Christians. They, like Christians today, often quoted the Bible; and by comparing their quotes with the manuscripts available today it can be seen that no really significant changes have taken place.

Cyprian was the bishop of Carthage; he died in AD 258. In his writings he quotes from the Old Testament over 740 times and from the New Testament 1,030 times. However, even before the days of Cyprian, i.e. within less than 200 years from the time of writing, over 30,000 New Testament quotes can be catalogued. They all testify to the reliability of the New Testament. The quotes are as follows:

Writer	Date (AD)	Gospels	Acts	Letters	Rev.	Total
Justin Martyr	133	268	10	49	3	330
Irenaeus	170	1,038	194	522	65	1,819
Clement of Alexandria	150-212	1,017	44	1,344	11	2,406
Tertullian	160-220	3,822	502	2,729	205	7,258
Hippolytus	170-235	734	42	414	188	1,378
Origen	185-253	9,231	349	8,177	165	17,922
Totals		16,110	1,141	13,225	637	31,113

The figures are obtainable from Geisler and Nix, *A General Introduction to the Bible*. To these we could add the writings of Eusebius (AD 263-

339). He quoted the New Testament 5,176 times (Gospels 3,258; Acts 211; Epistles 1,680; Revelation 27). This gives a total of over 36,000 quotations (over 37,000 if we include Cyprian) made within 250-300 years of the completion of the New Testament. But that does not complete the list. We have quoted just the main sources. We could add the writings of Augustine, Jerome, Gaius Romanus, Amabius, and many others. All these quotations show great harmony with the Greek manuscripts we have today; few show any significant difference. In *Can I Trust the Bible?*, Howard Vos states:

> From the standpoint of literary evidence the only logical conclusion is that the case for the reliability of the New Testament is infinitely stronger than that for any other record of antiquity.

Point 6 – The texts may be accurate but did all the events take place?

In the first five points of this second chapter it *has* been shown that, as near as really matters, we have the original text of the Bible. If that book was merely fiction, then for the writers to have gone to such lengths would have been absurd. If that book contains solely philosophy then, although we should want to discover as accurately as possible the original views propounded, the first five points need not have been so detailed. The Bible, however, contains not only philosophies about life and death, but also records of events, important events. Did these events take place – exactly as described? Are the descriptions accurate? Does the Bible contain historical fact, or is it one of those confusing historical fictions? If the events in it are not described accurately or did not even take place, then textual accuracy, dealt with in the first five points, is irrelevant. But if the historical detail described is accurate, factual, and true, then textual accuracy is essential to ensure the preservation of the truth.

Now it would be impossible, and unwise, to deal with every criticism which has been raised against the Bible, but two of the main ones may be summarized as follows:

(1) If an event is recorded in the Bible, but there is *no* evidence for it in other ancient records, then it did not take place and the writer of that part of the Bible made it up.

(2) If some aspect of an event described in the Bible is different from that given in other ancient records, then the Bible account is the one in error. The other records are the correct ones.

The first criticism can only be described as 'silly' and the second as 'illogical'. The textual accuracy of the Bible has been shown to be far superior to that of other ancient writings, and thus more weight should be given to it. More sensible criticisms would be:

(1) If an event is recorded in the Bible, but there is no evidence for it in other ancient records, then other evidence, manuscript and archaeological, should be sought for in the relevant area. In the light of any new discoveries, judgment can then be made on the biblical records of that event.

(2) If the detail of what has been recorded in the Bible is different from that of other ancient records, then the Bible record *may* be wrong, but so too may the other ancient records – and they are more likely to be wrong because of less manuscript support. Again more evidence, manuscript and archaeological, should be sought to enable judgment to be made.

What are the events which have been subjected to criticisms (1) and (2)? As examples, we proceed to deal in detail with two such criticisms, both of which concern Luke's writings in the New Testament.

1. LUKE 2:1-5. FACT OR FICTION?

In those days Caesar Augustus issued a decree that a census should be taken of the entire Roman world. (This was the first census that took place while Quirinius was governor of Syria.) And everyone went to his own town to register. So Joseph also went up from the town of Nazareth in Galilee to Judea, to Bethlehem the town of David, because he belonged to the house and line of David. He went there to register with Mary, who was pledged to be married to him and was expecting a child.

So begins one of the best known and best loved Christmas passages. Is it fiction? Did it take place? Some critics have said that here Luke blundered and got his facts wrong, or that he invented the whole thing. The critics cite four points to support their arguments:

(a) Augustus did not issue a decree ordering a census.
(b) There was no regular census under the Roman Empire.
(c) When a casual census did take place, the presence of the *wife was not required*, neither was the husband obliged to go to his original home.
(d) Cyrenius (Quirinius) did not govern Syria until AD 5 or 6, and the events described in Luke 2:1-5 are supposed to have taken place in about 4 BC.

If such criticisms are true then clearly Luke, and his Gospel and his Acts of the Apostles, are discredited. Sir William Ramsay claimed:

If an author can be guilty of any such perversions of history as have been attributed to the writer of Luke 2:1-5, he cannot deserve the rank and name of historian.

But note the '*if*'. Sir William Ramsay himself undertook excavations, and discovered at Antioch in Syria a stone on which Cyrenius is named. The date of that stone was given as between 10 BC and 7 BC, thus showing that Cyrenius was governing Syria before AD 5.

Another person named on the same stone was Servilius who had been governing Galatia in the years 8-7 BC. Therefore, without doubt, by 7 BC Cyrenius was governor of Syria. (See Appendix 2 for more details of this point.) So Luke was correct here; but what about the other three points?

As long ago as 1898, the British Museum published a volume dealing with the papyri discovered in Egypt, and this contained over two hundred documents dating from 10 BC to AD 75. In these writings it is shown that the Roman census was a *regular event*, and therefore such a census would have been carried out under Caesar Augustus. Thus criticisms (1) and (2) are unfounded. But what about Mary accompanying Joseph? One of these Egyptian documents states (our italics):

> The enrolment by *household* being at hand, it is necessary to notify all who for any cause so ever are outside their homes, to *return to their domestic hearths,* that they may accomplish the customary dispensation of enrolment and continue steadfastly in husbandry that belongeth to them.

The *household* is not just the husband! Also, that household was obliged to return to its original home. Thus criticism (3), like the others, is unfounded. Luke is shown to be completely accurate and trustworthy.

2. BUT DIDN'T LUKE MAKE MISTAKES IN THE ACTS OF THE APOSTLES?

In Acts 13:7 we read of Sergius Paulus who was 'proconsul' (*NIV*) of Cyprus. In 1912 Sir William Ramsay brought to light a block of stone bearing a Latin inscription which stated:

> To L[ucius] Sergius Paullus the younger, Son of Lucius, one of four commissioners in charge of the Roman streets, tribune of the soldiers of the sixth legion.

Here there is no mention of his being pro-consul, and here the name is spelt with double 'l'. Has Luke got his facts wrong? Couldn't he even spell the name right?

Certain critics maintained that Sergius Paullus was not a proconsul but a pro-praetor.

Pro-consul: Governor of a Roman Province i.e. a territory outside of Italy, and under Roman control.

Pro-praetor: Ex-praetor, with authority of praetor in a province not under military control.

Such differences may be lost on the majority of us, but ... who is right? Luke or his critics?

A coin found in Cyprus bears the inscription: 'In the proconsulship of Paulus'. Luke is right. Paulus was pro-consul and ... note the spelling; one '1.' The inscription discovered by Sir William gave the Latin spelling; Luke in Acts gave the Greek spelling.

We could go on and give detail after detail, but we shall just quickly deal with a few other points to show how archaeological discoveries have verified even the minutest details recorded by Luke in the Acts of the Apostles.

Acts 11:28 mentions that a famine was to happen in the days of Claudius Caesar! Did it occur? In the Pembroke collection there is a coin which bears the name Claudius Caesar. On one side is a bushel measure, and on the other a pair of scales – a well-recognized symbol for famine.

Acts 12:20-23 records the death of Herod as having taken place when he was arrayed in royal apparel, i.e. at some special event. Josephus, in *Antiquities* 19, 8, 2, records that Herod died during a festival held in honour of Claudius, but what was he wearing? Was it royal apparel? "He put on a garment made wholly of silver, and of a contexture truly wonderful, and came into the theatre early in the morning; at which time the silver of his garment being illuminated by the fresh reflection of the sun's rays, shone out after a surprising manner, and was so resplendent as to spread horror over those that looked intently upon him."

Acts 14:11, 12 links together, at Lycaonia, the Roman gods Jupiter and Mercury; (*KJV*; the *NIV* has the Greek equivalents Zeus and Hermes). A strange combination? No! Sir William Ramsay discovered a statue dedicated by the Lycaonians to these two gods, showing that Jupiter and Mercury were classed together in that local cult. Again this shows not only Luke's accurate knowledge of local affairs, but also his accurate recording of it.

Acts 17:6, 8 mentions 'city officials', literally 'politarchs'. This exact word may be read on an inscription taken from Thessalonica, which is in the possession of the British Museum. Luke is again absolutely correct with his titles, but until that discovery he was thought to be in the wrong, as the word 'politarch' does not occur in classical Greek literature. More recent discoveries have uncovered nineteen inscriptions bearing that title, and five of these relate to Thessalonica, the city referred to in Acts 17.

Acts 19:31 mentions 'officials of the province', literally 'Asiarch'. This exact title may be read on a slab taken from Ephesus. *Luke never makes a mistake. Wherever, and whenever, his account can be tested against other ancient finds, it is always found to be accurate.*

Acts 19:35 mentions that "the city of Ephesus is the *guardian of the temple* of the great Artemis." An inscription dug up at Ephesus speaks of the city as 'the first and greatest metropolis of Asia and twice *temple keeper* of the Emperor': exactly the same word!

Acts 28:7 refers to Publius as the chief man of Malta; literally 'the first man'. Inscriptions have been unearthed which give just that very title, 'the first man'.

We could go on, but there is little point in saying more. Surely we have demonstrated the case. As Charles H. Welch claims, in *True from the Beginning:*

Every turn of the spade that brings forth the hidden testimony has confirmed the truth of the Bible narrative. The reader has not yet seen the following headline in the press:

GREAT ARCHAEOLOGICAL DISCOVERY
BIBLE PROVED UNTRUE

and we do not believe we ever will.

Point 7 – What about the Old Testament?

It is true to say that the Old Testament raises many more questions, in the minds of most people, than does the New. Thus it would seem sensible if we dealt with a few more criticisms in depth. In doing so we shall not concern ourselves solely with the detailed, often miniscule queries of the scholarly critics, but we shall also consider those issues which raise themselves in the minds of most people. We shall start near the end of the Old Testament and work our way towards the beginning, towards Genesis, towards that most interesting and challenging section of the Bible.

(1) BELSHAZZAR – DID HE EXIST?

Belshazzar, king of Babylon, is mentioned in Daniel 5:1-2; but, when his name was not found in the records of Babylon, great doubt was thrown upon the reliability of the book of Daniel. However, more recent archaeological discoveries have changed all that. There is a clay cylinder, from a temple in Babylon, and now in the British Museum, which bears the following prayer:

> In the heart of Belshazzar, my first-born son, the offspring of my loins, set the fear of thine exalted godhead, so that he may be satisfied with the fulness of life.

But that's not all. Another discovery uncovered large earthenware vases containing 3,000 to 4,000 contracts, which were the securities of the Babylonian bank called 'Sons of Egibi' which operated from 1000 to 400 BC. Among the recorded transactions was a letter to 'the secretary of Belshazzar, son of the King'. Further, another transaction recorded that Belshazzar owned a sheep farm.

(2) WHEN DOES 300 = 800?

2 Kings 18:14 records that the Jewish King, Hezekiah, had to pay the King of Assyria 300 talents of silver. The archaeological discovery of the Cylinder of Sennacharib threw doubt on this, for it recorded that the King

of Assyria received 800 talents of silver from Hezekiah. Which is correct? The Bible or the Cylinder of Sennacharib? Answer – both, because other evidence has shown that the Assyrian talent of silver was equal to three-eights of the Palestinian talent of silver. Exchange rates existed then, as now!

(3) DID THE WALLS OF JERICHO COME TUMBLING DOWN?

Joshua 6:5 and 6:20 record that the walls of the city 'fell down flat' (*KJV*). A better translation would be 'collapsed'. Did the walls of Jericho collapse? Professor John Garstang excavated Jericho and wrote (*Joshua and Judges*):

> As to the main fact, then, there remains no doubt: the walls fell outwards so completely that the attackers would be able to clamber up and over their ruins into the city.

Why was this so unusual? Simply because the walls of cities do not usually fall outwards, they fall inwards, yet we read in Joshua 6:20:

> The wall collapsed; so every man charged straight in, and they took the city.

Garstang's discovery confirms this, and even more. He went on to write:

> Every room in the palace area tells the same tale of walls half fallen, reddened by fire, amid layers of white ashes and ashes of charcoal ... While pottery has been found in abundance in Jericho, so far no vessel of bronze or other metal has been found. Yet such perishable stuffs as burnt wheat, lentils, onions, etc. have been discovered. The absence of any metal vessels is explained by the statement in Joshua 6:24, where we read, "And they burnt the city with fire, and all that was therein: only the silver, and the gold, and the vessels of brass and iron, they put into the treasury of the house of the Lord."

Here the Bible solved the archaeologist's dilemma!

(4) WAS MOSES EVER IN EGYPT?

Some have doubted whether Moses was ever in Egypt, but this criticism has been refuted by Dr. A. S. Yahuda, ex-professor of Medieval Hebrew Literature at the University of Madrid, He has demonstrated, beyond doubt, that the man who wrote most of Genesis and Exodus – that is Moses – had an intimate acquaintance with ancient Egypt, its people and its language. All this evidence is presented in his book *The Language of the Pentateuch in its Relation to Egypt,* which involves the use of Hebrew type, and a knowledge of Hebrew and Egyptian grammar.

(5) ABRAHAM AND THE KINGS OF GENESIS 14.
FACT OR FICTION?

Doubt had been cast upon the very existence of such kings as Amraphel, King of Shinar; Arioch, King of Ellasar and Chedorlaomer, King of Elam – all mentioned in Genesis 14:1. In 1902, M. J. de Morgan discovered, in Susa in Persia, the ancient law code known as the Code of Hammurabi. This Hammurabi was King of Babylon, and the law code – for which the latest date is 2100 BC – governed an area from the Persian Gulf to the Caspian Sea, and from Persia to the Mediterranean. Thus it was in force throughout the land of Canaan, through which Abraham travelled. Now there are some who uphold the view that Hammurabi, King of Babylon, is the same person as Amraphel, King of Shinar (Shinar being another name of Babylon). In Illustrations of Old Testament History, D. J. Wiseman states that "the identification of Amraphel with Hammurabi is no longer likely." However, inscriptions at Susa assert the existence of Chedorlaomer and the dominance of Elam, as recorded in Genesis 14; and Arioch, King of Ellasar, is found in those inscriptions as 'Eri-Aku, King of Larsa'.

Abraham had dealings with all these people, yet we read that Abraham's very existence has been questioned. The nineteenth-century German critic, Wellhausen, said of Abraham:

> We may not regard him as a historical person, he might with more likelihood be regarded as a free creation of unconscious art.

Which is but a polite way of saying that Abraham never existed! But was he a fictional character? Max Burrows thinks not (*What Mean these Stones?*):

> Everything indicates that here we have a historical individual ... he is not mentioned in any known archaeological source, but his name appears in Babylonia as a personal name in the very period to which he belongs.

Charles H. Welch, in his book already quoted, agrees with Burrows:

> Moreover, in the Assyrian Eponym canon, written in Abraham's day in Abraham's land, is found the very name *Aburamu*. Every investigation brings further and fuller conviction that the record of the life of Abraham is a record of fact.

(6) THE TOWER OF BABEL – THAT MUST BE A MYTH?

Genesis 11 records the building of the tower of Babel. Years later, in about 600-550 BC, that land was ruled by the famous king Nebuchadnezzar, who built a magnificent city at Babylon. However this king also took an interest in renovating and preserving antique buildings.

At Borsippa a series of cylinders was found, one of which recorded the rebuilding of an ancient tower:

> The temple of the seven lights of the earth, the tower of Borsippa, which the former king [or most ancient king] had erected and had completed to a height of 42 yards whose pinnacle, however, he had not set up, since remote days had fallen into ruin ... As it was ages before I built it anew; as it was in remote days, I erected its pinnacle.

A tower that could be said, at Nebuchadnezzar's time, to belong to 'remote days' and to have been erected by 'the most ancient king' must be ancient indeed. This may well refer to the tower of Babel which, as Genesis 11:8 records, was left unfinished and here we read that the 'pinnacle' had not been set up.

Also Genesis 11:3 states that the bricks used were 'burnt thoroughly' and that 'slime [bitumen] was used for mortar'. Examination of the bricks pile at Borsippa shows this to be the case.

A third testimony to the tower of Babel is found on a bronze doorstep at the British Museum. This exhibit was taken from the temple of Birs Nimrod, which was built upon completion of the restoration of the Tower of Babel. The doorstep commemorated that restoration.

We could go on and give many more detailed descriptions, but instead we shall quickly give a few more archaeological discoveries which have demonstrated the accuracy of the Old Testament, even in its minutest detail.

2 KINGS 10:29-32 records how the Jewish King, Jehu, was defeated by Hazael, King of Damascus. This is verified by the *Black Obelisk*, a tapering shaft of black marble, now in the British Museum, which shows Jehu paying tribute to Hazael.

2 KINGS 3:4 records details of Mesha, King of Moab, who is also the subject of the *Moabite Stone*.

THE BOOK OF JOSHUA records how the Jewish people advanced into the land of Canaan. Many cities of that country, and of Egypt, are named; and the book uses the words *El* and *Jehovah* as names of God. The *Tell-el-Armarna Tablets* show that the cities named in the book of Joshua are exactly as named. The tablets also record that correspondence was carried on between Canaan and Egypt, and that Canaan was in great fear of being invaded – by Joshua. They also show that the names of *El* and *Jehovah* were used of God at that time. What testimony to support the writings of Joshua!

EXODUS 1:11 records that the Jews, as slaves, built the Egyptian cities of Pithom and Ramses; and that, on the banks of the Nile, these people were forced to make the bricks required. Archaeological work at the sites of Pithom and Ramses has unearthed bricks made of Nile mud.

GENESIS 41:14 records that, in Egypt, "Joseph shaved himself"; and archaeological digs have uncovered razors from that time and place.

Surely the reader will, by now, be convinced of the reliability of the bulk of the Bible. Many of the items mentioned above are in the British Museum, but not all are on display.

Point 8 – Weren't they Aunt Sallies?

In points 6 and 7 a number of issues have been raised and answered, but these were not Aunt Sallies set up for the sole purpose of knocking down. No! All the issues raised were, at one time, adverse criticisms of the Bible which the Bible student could not answer, and some are still being discussed even though the evidence takes the issue beyond dispute. The interesting feature of the subject matter in points 6 and 7 is that, with *the passage of time*, archaeological discoveries have shown the Bible to be correct. This is an important principle. Adverse criticisms of the Bible which cannot be satisfactorily answered today may well be easily dismissed in twenty or thirty years time. Fresh evidence is constantly coming to light which supports the Biblical accounts. Theories may often clash with the Bible record, but verifiable facts have never yet done so.

We end this chapter by giving details of a number of subjects which are, at present, under discussion and over which experts disagree, including giants, the flood and the creation / evolution debate. There is some evidence to support the biblical view – but is it enough? Bearing in mind all that has been discovered to support items listed in points 6 and 7, it would appear that in time more evidence will be found to support the biblical view of these subjects. Anyway, only time will tell. The interested reader can decide for himself if he wishes to read the books recommended on these controversial subjects.

(1) WHO WROTE WHAT AND WHEN?

The key book in dating the writings of the New Testament is the Acts of the Apostles, written by Luke. If that book can be dated accurately then the other writings can be dated relative to it.

King Aretas is mentioned in 2 Corinthians 11:32-33, which deals with Paul's escape from Damascus, an event also mentioned in Acts 9:23-25. Aretas was the king of the Nabataeans, a region east of Judea. He lived from 9 BC to AD 40, but between AD 37 and 54 there are no Damascus coins bearing the Roman Emperor's image. It seems that Gaius granted the city of Damascus to Aretas in AD 37 (see page 81, *New Bible Dictionary*, second edition). This suggests that the incident of Paul escaping with his life from Damascus took place between AD 37 and 40. However, there are events which we can date more accurately than this.

Acts 12:21-23 records the death of Herod, and from secular history it can be ascertained when that happened. Herod, according to history, started to reign not many days after the accession of Caligula (who is also known as Gaius) which took place on 16 March AD 37, Caligula was murdered on 24 January AD 41, and on the accession of Claudius, Herod was made king over Judea and Samaria (see Josephus, *Antiquities* 19, 8, 2).

Josephus also records that Herod died during a festival held in honour of Claudius, who had been in Britain for six months and returned to Rome in January AD 44. This festival was held later that year in Caesarea, the Roman capital of Palestine. Thus Acts 12:21-23 can be fixed with certainty at AD 44. Events such as these allow the rest of the book of Acts to be dated to the required degree of accuracy. Similarly the other books of the New Testament can be dated by reference to the book of Acts, and other historical details.

However, some critics claim that certain of the epistles were not written by the people to whom they were attributed. For example, some say Peter did not write his second epistle but someone else wrote it about two hundred years later and used Peter's name to get authority for it. Or again, many expositors take the view that Paul did not write Hebrews.

In point 7, it was pointed out that the *language* of Genesis and Exodus proved beyond doubt that the writer of these books had been in Egypt, and was well acquainted with the country, the people, their ideas and language. Language is a great ally in the field of dating. As far back as 1863 Bishop Lightfoot wrote:

> If we could only recover letters that ordinary people wrote to each other without any thought of being literary, we should have the greatest possible help for the understanding of the language of the New Testament generally.

Not only would such a discovery help in the understanding but it would be of vital importance with respect to dating. The language of nineteenth century Britain is very different from that of the seventeenth century. Gone, for instance, are the 'thees' and 'thous', and the '-eth' and 'est' endings of the verbs. Similarly writings of two hundred years ago could never be confused with the writings of today. The language and style are so different.

Over the years, many interesting discoveries have been uncovered in the dry sands of Egypt, so good at preserving ancient documents. Contracts, letters, petitions, deeds and census returns, as well as a public notice and a will, have been found. These documents were written between 150 BC and AD 150, and so employ the very language and style of that time. It is this language and style that is used in the New Testament. Thus there can be little doubt that the second epistle of Peter was written in the first century AD. Critics wishing to give it a date two hundred years later have the testimony of language to overcome.

But as for Paul writing Hebrews – in *The Christian Herald,* Marcus Beverley wrote the following, in a review of *Perfection or Perdition?*, a commentary on Hebrews by Stuart Allen and Charles H. Welch, which advocates the Pauline authorship of Hebrews:

> The discussion on the authorship of the Epistles is sound and comprehensive. This particular section, of considerable length, is contributed by Stuart Allen and is one of the most satisfying, from the Evangelical standpoint, that has been written for years.

The authorship, admittedly, presents problems. Origen's summary still holds good: Who wrote the Epistle, God only knows certainly! Mr. Allen leans to the suggestion that the thought is Pauline, and that the amanuensis was Luke or possibly Silas. It is certainly an impressive fact that the Eastern Church decided that the Letter was the Apostle Paul's.

Some of the evidence presented in *Perfection or Perdition?* is again a comparison of language. One example is that Hebrews ends with "Grace be with you all," and Paul is the only New Testament writer to end his writings with a reference to 'grace'. Those interested in the authorship of Hebrews may care to read the book and weigh the issues for themselves. Another interesting view on the authorship of Hebrews and 2 Peter is found on pages 37-41 of *Number in Scripture* by Dr. E. W. Bullinger.

Some have suggested that the prophecy of Daniel was written hundreds of years later than it claims, during the time of Antiochus Epiphanes or later. This would mean that the prophecy was not in fact a prophecy, stating what was to happen, but a history couched in prophetic terms. Sir Robert Anderson in his book *Daniel in the Critics' Den* shows by language, and other arguments, that it was written earlier and is a genuine prophecy.

Another typical dispute in this area is the dating of the Epistle to the Galatians. Some would hold that the epistle was written to the Kingdom of Galatia, which was situated north-east of Asia Minor (modern Turkey) and constituted a broad strip of land over 200 miles in length. Its chief cities were Tavium, Ancyra and Pessinus. If this view is correct then Paul founded the churches there on his second missionary journey, mentioned in Acts 16:6. This would imply that the Epistle was written after the Council of Jerusalem, recorded in Acts 15, but no mention of that Council's decisions is made in the Galatian epistle. This is, indeed, extraordinary, for those decisions would have supported Paul's view that Gentile Christians need not be circumcised nor keep the Law of Moses. Thus some have concluded that the Jerusalem Council either did not take place, or took place at a different time! Either way, they say Luke was wrong! But there is a simpler solution to this problem, as the two maps which follow illustrate.

Others hold the view that the Epistle was written to the *Province* of Galatia which, in addition to the kingdom, went southwards to include Lycaonia, Phrygia, and a portion of Pisidia in which lay Antioch, Lystra and Derbe.

If this view is correct, then Paul formed these churches while on his first missionary journey, and a second visit is mentioned in Acts 14:21 on his return journey. This would imply that the Galatian epistle was written before the Jerusalem Council of Acts 15, and then no inconsistency is introduced into Luke's writings.

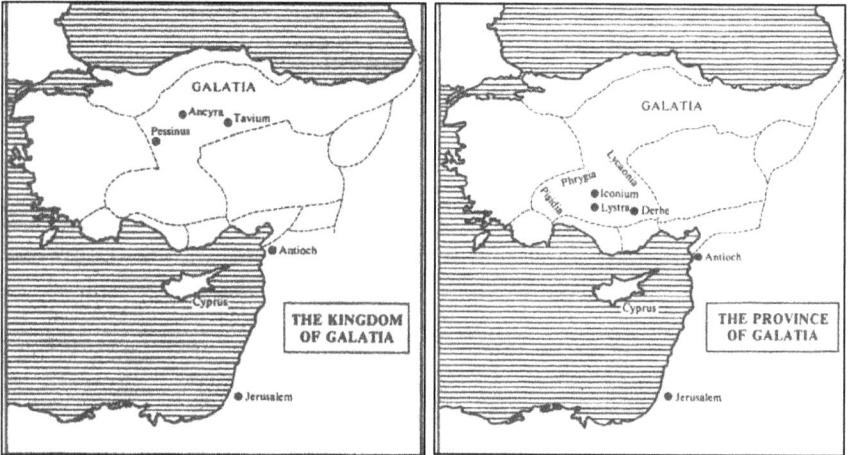

But let's return to some of the Old Testament problems.

(2) THE WHOLE EARTH WAS OF ONE LANGUAGE, AND OF ONE SPEECH

Genesis 11:1 records that the whole earth had one language. Such a statement was heatedly refuted at one time; but in *Archaeology and Bible History,* Joseph Free mentions that some modern-day philologists attest to the likelihood of such an origin for the world's languages.

Alfredo Trombetti says he can trace and prove the common origin of *all* languages. Max Mueller also attests to the common origin. And Otto Jespersen goes so far to say that language was directly given to the first men by God.

It should be said that this view is not shared by all philologists, but Arthur Custance, in his *Doorway Paper 'Who taught Adam to speak?'* deals with the significant problem that language can only be learnt by hearing it at a very young age from someone speaking to you. He considers cases of feral children with no language, and who struggle at a later age to develop significant language skills. So ... who taught humans to speak?

(3) THE FLOOD – LOCAL OR UNIVERSAL?

It was considered impossible that a flood – as recorded in Genesis chapters 6 to 9 – could have occurred. In the first part of this century, such passages of the Bible were treated with caution; but in 1928-29, Dr. C. L. Woolley carried out extensive excavations at Ur of the Chaldees. He wrote:

> The shafts went deeper, and suddenly the character of the soil changed. Instead of the stratified pottery and rubbish, we were in perfectly clean clay, uniform throughout, the texture of which showed that it had been laid there by water ... The clean clay continued without change until it had attained a thickness of a little over eight feet. Then, as suddenly as it had began, it stopped, and we were once more in layers of rubbish ... No ordinary rising of the rivers would leave behind it anything approaching the bulk of this bank; eight feet of sediment imply a very great depth of water, and the flood which deposited it must have been of a magnitude unparalleled in local history.

Dr. Woolley also wrote to *The Times,* and his letter was published on 16 March 1929:

> The Sumerians regarded the Flood as a historical event, marking an epoch in their national annals... He would have been an optimist

indeed who had hoped to produce material evidence for such an event as the Flood of the Sumerian legend, which is also the Flood of the Book of Genesis: but in no other way can I interpret the facts which our excavations here give us.

Another letter appeared in *The Times*, this one from Dr. Stephen Langdon, Professor of Assyriology at Oxford University. He wrote concerning his discoveries at Kish:

In this layer are two precipitations of clay, potsherd, and stranded fish lying perfectly horizontally. They could not have been placed there by the hand of man, and their position in the layer cannot possibly be explained by any other hypothesis than that of a flood over that part of Mesopotamia ... We were loath to believe that we had obtained confirmation of the Deluge of Genesis, but there is no doubt about it now.

But had Woolley and Langdon found evidence for the *universal* flood of Genesis? Some suggested they had, but in the years that followed other experts disputed that. However, it should be noted that in the quotations given above, Dr. Woolley used the phrase, 'unparalleled in *local* history', and Dr. Langdon wrote 'a flood over *that part of Mesopotamia*'. Thus the compromise view of the experts seemed to be that here was evidence of a great flood over part of Mesopotamia (modern Iraq, the area around the rivers Tigris and Euphrates).

So was Genesis talking about a *local* flood or a *universal* flood? The problem is caused by language. For example, in Daniel 2:39 we read of a third kingdom, the one of bronze, which was to 'rule over the whole earth'. Now whether this was Greece or Rome matters not; neither ruled over the 'whole' earth. However, as far as the people of those areas were concerned, it was 'the whole earth'. Similarly, Nebuchadnezzar addressed the citizens of his kingdom as "To the people, nations and men of every language, who live in *all the world"* (Daniel 4:1). Yet his kingdom was smaller than either the Greek or Roman empires.

Thus we must be careful with words that may have a universal meaning. We will often ask such questions as 'Is everyone here?' but we do not mean everyone in the world. We have in mind a clearly defined sub-group. So was it a local flood or a universal flood?[4]

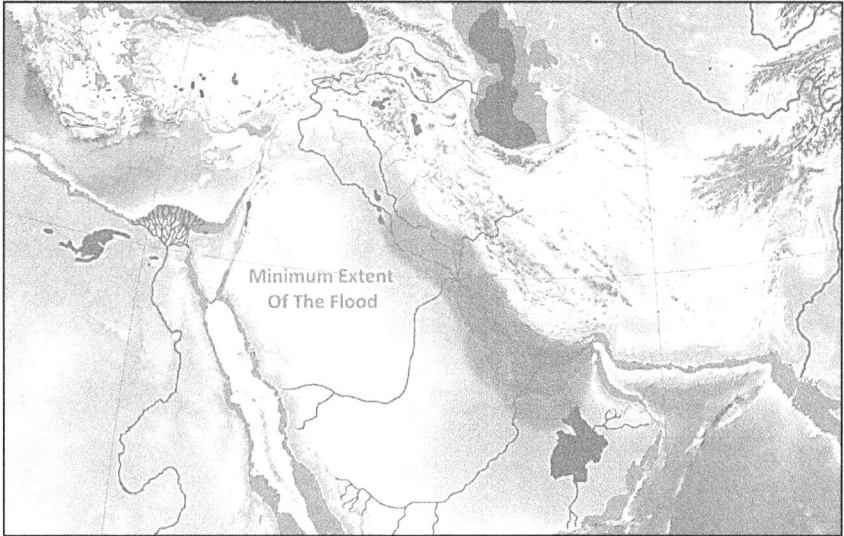

Minimum Extent
Of The Flood

That a flood took place is beyond dispute. Discovery of the Babylonian flood tablets added more evidence for a flood. These were found at Nineveh; and, recorded on twelve stone tablets, was the Epic of Gilgamesh which described an ancient flood. Was it the same one as described in Genesis? Was it universal?

Mr. H. Weld-Blundell purchased in Baghdad some cuneiform tablets for the Ashmolean Museum in Oxford. On the prism catalogued W. B. 444 are 379 lines, many giving lists of kings from the earliest times. Two interesting lines are:

Line 39 – The Deluge came up
Line 40 – After the Deluge had come

---

[4] For discussion of this issue see *Noah's Flood* by Sylvia Penny, published by the Open Bible Trust.

A flood is now undisputed; but was it universal? Much work has gone on in many parts of the world to try and ascertain if the Genesis flood is local or universal. In *Earth in Upheaval*, Immanuel Velikovsky reports evidence of this flood in various parts of Britain, for example at Kirkdale in Yorkshire, Cefn in Wales, Bleadon in Somerset, Brentford near London and in the Thames Valley. In *Myths and Miracles*, David Watson adds Scotland, Java, China and Africa. Evidence has also been found in France and the U.S.A. However, did all this flooding take place at the same time? The person who wants a detailed discussion of the 'local flood versus universal flood' issue should read *The Genesis Flood* by Whitcomb and Morris and *Noah's Flood* by Sylvia Penny.

Before leaving the issue of the Genesis Flood, there is one further interesting phenomenon which should be brought to the reader's attention. Genesis 8:4 records that the ark came to rest "upon the mountains of Ararat". In the nineteenth century, a shepherd's story prompted an expedition to climb Mount Ararat, in Turkey, near the border with the former U.S.S.R.

At the foot of Mount Ararat lies the small village of Bayzit, whose inhabitants had for generations recounted the remarkable experience of a shepherd who was said to have seen a great wooden ship on the mountain. Werner Keller mentions this in *The Bible as History*. He goes on:

> A report from a Turkish expedition in 1833 seemed to confirm the shepherd's story, since it mentioned a wooden prow of a ship which in the summer season stuck out of the south glacier.

> The next person to claim to have seen it was Dr. Nouri, Archdeacon of Jerusalem and Babylon. This agile ecclesiastical dignitary undertook a journey in 1892 to discover the source of the Euphrates.[5] On his return he told of the wreckage of a ship in the eternal ice: 'The interior was full of snow: the outer wall was of a red colour.'

---

[5] Note: he did not go looking for the ark.

During the First World War, a Russian flying officer by name Roskowitzki announced he had spotted from his plane 'the remains of wreckage of a fair sized ship' on the south flank of Ararat. Although it was in the middle of war, Tsar Nicholas II dispatched a search party without delay. It was supposed not only to have seen the ship, but even to have photographed it. All proof of this however perished, presumably in the Revolution.

From the Second World War there are likewise several cases of aerial observation. They come from a Russian pilot, and from four American flyers. These latter reports brought into the field the American historian and missionary, Dr. Aaron Smith of Greensborough, an expert on the Flood. As a result of years of labour, he has collected a complete history of the literature of Noah's Ark. There are 80,000 works, in seventy-two languages, about the Flood; of which 70,000 mention the legendary wreckage of the Ark.

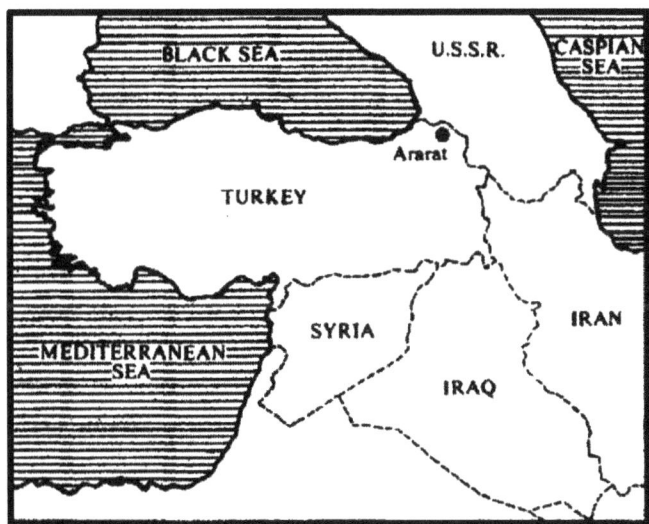

80,000 works in seventy two languages! That's a lot of reading! Over 70,000 of them mention the Ark on Ararat; the Secrets of the Lost Races by Rend Noorbergen gives some very up-to-date information on the subject.

(4) WHAT ABOUT THE GIANTS?

Genesis 6:4 states "There were giants in the earth in those days; and also after that" (*KJV*). In Numbers 13:33 the spies reported that they had seen "giants, the sons of Anak, which come of the giants".

Giants are also mentioned in Deuteronomy 2:10-21, Joshua 12:1-4 and 2 Samuel 21:15-22; but the most famous of all was Goliath (1 Samuel 17:4), who was killed by the shepherd boy David, who used just a pebble and a sling. Is this true? Is it a fairy tale? Did giants live on the earth?
If we delve into the ancient folklore of many countries, we find stories of giants, no doubt greatly distorted from the original events, but containing a germ of truth. Stories of giants can be found in such countries as Wales and Ireland and France. Children's tales, which often had truth at the start, are full of such people – but what does the Bible mean by a giant?

2 Samuel 21:20 describes a giant having six fingers on each hand and six toes on each foot. This would imply some kind of mutation, but how big were they? In 1 Samuel 17:4, Goliath is said to be, in height, 'six cubits and a span', which most experts take to be about 9-12 feet, depending on how they understand the cubit. In Deuteronomy 3:11, the bed of the giant Og, king of Bashan, is said to be nine cubits in length and four cubits in breadth. It is said to be made of iron and to lie in Rabbath. Thus giants should not be looked upon as being as tall as 30 or 40 feet, but as less than double normal size.

But apart from the Bible and ancient folklore, is there any other evidence for giants? Archaeological discoveries at Bashan, home of the giant king Og, have uncovered a city in which everything is approximately double size. *The Giant Cities of Bashan* by Rev. J. L. Porter is worth reading on this subject.

However, there is more modern-day evidence of giants, or giantism, as it is called nowadays. On February 28, 2011, BBC Radio 4 broadcast a programme on the subject. Earlier, in January of 2011, the *Mail* carried an article on the Skeleton of Charles Byrne, an 18th century Irish giant, who was over 8 feet tall; figures vary from 8 ft. 1 inch to 8 ft. 7 inches.

Latest research on the DNA from its teeth have been analysed and it has been suggested that such abnormal growth is due to a mutant gene. This may also have been the problem with Anna Haining Swan (born Bates). She was a female 7 ft. 6 inch giant from Nova Scotia in Canada, who lived between 1846 and 1888.

(5) HOW CAN THE SUN STAND STILL?

Joshua 10:13 records, "... So the sun stood still in the midst of heaven, and hasted not to go down about a whole day." (*KJV*). Did this happen?

If it did, then some parts of the earth must have had a very long night! In his book *Worlds in Collision,* Immanuel Velikovsky catalogues ancient writings which mention a very long day and others which record a very long night, but he also quotes one which refers to how the sun was caught on the horizon and took a very long time to break through.

Velikovsky's book deals with the account of Joshua's long day, and also covers the ten-degree movement of the sun mentioned in Isaiah 38:8.

(6) ONE LARGE CONTINENT?

"... Let the waters under heaven be gathered together unto one place, and let the dry *land* appear; ..." states Genesis 1:9 (*KJV*). Here it is evident that not only were the waters in one place but so too was the land. Such a statement was ridiculed by many geographers and geologists a hundred or more years ago, but the most magnificent *Readers Digest Atlas* has several diagrams on its early pages; the first of which shows the land gathered together in one place, and the last the present-day distribution. This is an illustration of the Continental Drift theory which has grown in popularity, and which is in harmony with Genesis 1:9. Some mathematicians, however, have stated that such a theory is untenable as there do not exist, within the world's framework, forces large enough to cause such a drift. Meanwhile geologists are showing how the various strata in the different continents, at the relevant points, *do* match up ... so who will win the battle?

One problem is that the mathematics used is based upon the theory of uniformity, that everything hundreds and thousands of years ago was more or less as it is now. All changes are therefore infinitesimal, and so significant changes occur over millions of years. Thus it is argued that, as no such forces exist today to cause such a movement of the continents, then no such forces existed in the past.

This theory of uniformity has been seriously challenged in such books as *Bombarded Earth* by René Gallant, and in *Earth in Upheaval* by Immanuel Velikovsky. The theory is also discussed in two previously mentioned books, *The Genesis Flood* and *Worlds in Collision*. These books show that the world is not infrequently subjected to external catastrophe; and, if this catastrophe element can be built into the mathematical model, then mathematicians may well find that there are forces large enough to cause the drift required by the geologists.

(7) CREATION OR EVOLUTION?

Cosmology is the study of the origin of the universe. One of the most brilliant scientists in this area is Dr. Jean Charon, a physicist at the French Atomic Energy Commission. His main research has involved unified field theory, and cosmological models. The opening words of his book, *Cosmology*, are:

> The question: 'Who created the world?' is apt to be embarrassing, even when put to an eminent modern scholar. The answer 'The world was created by God' would almost unanimously have been given several centuries ago, and even today this reply has not been replaced by anything much clearer.

Many people think that evolution has been 'proved beyond doubt', yet Jean Charon's words show this not to be the case, and there are others like him. Robert Boyd (1922-2004) was Professor of Astrophysics at University College, London. He wrote a poem entitled *Creation*, the opening lines of which are:

> The mystery of being, still unsolved,

By all our science and philosophy.

To men such as these, science has not provided the answers. However, we should stop awhile and ask ourselves what does Genesis 1 actually teach? In her book *Theories of Creation* (published by The Open Bible Trust), Sylvia Penny discusses the pros and cons of the five most popular interpretations. These are:

Biblical Interpretation	Scientific View
Non-literal	Theistic Evolution
Day-age theory	Progressive Creation
Six literal days creation	Scientific Creationism and the Young Earth view
The Gap theory	Ruin of the original creation – six days reconstruction
Creation revealed in six days	Can accommodate any of the above

Details of the last one, which suggests that God told Adam or Moses or someone certain facts about the creation on six separate days, can be found in P. J. Wiseman's book *Creation Revealed in Six Days*. Whether or not the Hebrew text can support that view is up to the reader to decide; but this view has the advantage that it takes Genesis 1 out of science, or should that be it takes science out of Genesis 1?

But returning to science, although modern day evolutionists, such as Richard Attenborough and Richard Dawkins, like to give the impression that evolution has been proved beyond doubt, there are people who are not convinced. To some, evolution is scientifically non-verifiable; i.e. it cannot be proved. Why is that?

True science relies upon the fact that the scientific theories (or mathematical models as some call them) can be tested by independent experiments, and either verified or disproved. This cannot be done with evolution theory.

Scientific procedure follows these five steps:

1. Real world observations.

2. Construct a Theory, or Mathematical Model.

3. Perform experiments based on the theory/model, and obtain experimental results.

4. Question? Do the experimental results based on the theory agree with the real world observations to the required degree of accuracy?

5. If 'Yes'; end; and the theory is accredited.

If 'No'; *either* refine the theory; i.e. make it more sophisticated/complicated, and go back to 3;*or* discard the theory, and construct a new theory/model, and start again at 2.

Experiments can be performed on many scientific theories, and the ones that pass the above procedure stand the test of time; e.g. ones such as Newton's Laws of Motion, Quantum Theory, Relativity, and the like. However, one cannot perform the above scientific procedure on the ideas of Richard Dawkins as to how this or that evolved, quite simply because it is impossible to perform any experiments to test his suggestions.

This would also be true of the theories put forward of Theistic Evolution, Progressive Creation, Scientific Creationism, Intelligent Design or the Gap Theory. We simply cannot go back in time; or recreate the situation as they suggest it was thousands or millions or billions of years ago. We cannot perform experiments and test to see if what they suggest did actually take place. Just like atheistic evolution, none are verifiable.

In fact, it is impossible to apply the scientific procedure outlined above to many explanations of the past. Not only that, experts in those fields can contradict one another, and their opinions often change. For example; there is a 400 year old mound in Shropshire; and at the present time there are four different views held about its origin and purpose, by differing archaeologists. Similarly with evolutionists, they can differ significantly with one another, as was seen some years ago in the heated debates which took place between those who held to Darwinian Evolution and those who thought Punctuated Evolution was better.

Again, if we consider the Minoan Civilisation based on Crete; the explanations of the eminent Sir Arthur Evans of the Ashmolean Museum in Oxford, given 100 years ago, are now disputed and disagreed with. And it is the same with evolutionists. They disagree with the ideas of earlier evolutionists; and, in spite of the forceful way in which Richard Dawkins puts forward his current views as to how thing evolved, we can be sure that in 100 years time few, if any, of his ideas will be credible. Such is the nature of evolution. It is not a tight and testable science, and there is a growing number of voices expressing opposition.

> Uncommon Descent holds that... Materialistic ideology has subverted the study of biological and cosmological origins; so that, the actual content of these sciences has become corrupted. The problem, therefore, is not merely that science is being used illegitimately to promote a materialistic worldview, but that this worldview is actively undermining scientific inquiry, and is leading to incorrect and unsupported conclusions about biological and cosmological origins. At the same time, intelligent design (ID) offers a promising scientific alternative to materialistic theories of biological and cosmological evolution – an alternative that is finding increasing theoretical and empirical support. Hence, it now needs to be vigorously developed as a scientific, intellectual, and cultural project. (*Uncommon Descent* web site)

The simple fact is that some science is not value-free, and this was the subject of an article in *The Guardian Weekly* on February 20, 2011. Written by Thomas Jackson, the sub-heading was "Dawkins does not realise that science in not value-free." Some of Dawkins' theories are simply his views and, as mentioned on the previous page, in the next 100 years many will be superseded.

The theories of climate change demonstrate well that some science is not value-free. Following two exceptionally hot British summers in 2006 and 2007, the climatologists told us that the country was getting warmer, and that we should start to cultivate Mediterranean plants. Then came three poor summers, one the cloudiest on the record; and December 2010 was the coldest December on record. The climatologists rapidly changed their minds and declared that the effect of global warming was that Britain would get colder!

Lastly, to demonstrate the strength of those who are not convinced by evolution, we mention the Creation Research Society of the USA. This is a research and publication society, and its voting membership is *limited to scientists having at least a master's degree in natural or applied science.*

The Society does not agree with evolution and it endorses the biblical record of creation. It has published a textbook for schools and colleges entitled *Biology: a search for order in complexity.*

Along with this textbook goes teachers' guide, and teachers' and students' laboratory manuals. This is a society for highly qualified scientists, not a society of amateurs. They publicize many of the problems and flaws in evolution theory; but their explanations as to how God created suffers from the same problem as we mentioned earlier – their theories cannot be verified, because we cannot replicate the situation as it was then and perform the experiments. (Appendix 3 contains more details of organisations which support some form of Divine Creation, including Intelligent Design.)

In conclusion, consider the quote from Tom Stoppard's *Jumpers*. George, the professor of philosophy, states

> Still, at least in the Judaeo-Christian tradition, nothing is heard either of a God who created the universe and then washed his hands of it, or, alternatively, a God who merely took a comparatively recent interest in the chance produce of universal gasses.

Thus a core belief of Christianity is that God created. How he did so, and when he did so, may be beyond and above us; and Christians do differ on their detailed interpretation of Genesis chapter 1.

However, I have been asked by an evolutionist as to whether I really believe God created man from the dust of the earth. My reply was to ask him if he really believed man evolved from rain on a rock. Both of those statements are very similar, but neither can be proved, and each is accepted by faith. I cannot prove to anyone that God created, but I believe that he did. And it is good that some evolutionists are admitting that evolution cannot be proved, but that they 'believe' in it.

However, here we have a massive subject on which hundreds of books have been written, and hundreds more will be written. It is an issue which will never be settled – for an atheistic, unbelieving world can never allow a Creator, since belief in a Creator would imply a moral response. Thus the theory of evolution is philosophical by nature, and will continue to be so. In fact, it is much more philosophical than it is scientific! It removes the maker/creator, and thus removes man's responsibility to him. This has appealed to many, such as the philosopher Aldous Huxley who, summarising the views of many, wrote:

> I had motives for not wanting the world to have meaning; consequently assumed that it had been none, and was able without any difficulty to find satisfying reasons for this assumption ... For myself, as, no doubt, for most of my contemporaries, the philosophy of meaningless was essentially an instrument of liberation. The liberation we desired was simultaneously liberation from a certain political and economic system and liberation from a certain system of morality. We objected to morality because it interfered with our sexual freedom.

This appeared in the *Report* in June 1966, and in 1967 censorship was abolished and pornography became legal.

A Reliable Book.
Well Worth Studying

RELIABLE – of sound and consistent character or quality; trustworthy; honest; credible.

In our investigations we have shown the Bible to be credible. The writers of its books have been shown to be honest in what they have recorded. The whole book is trustworthy, and is of sound and consistent character. It is not historical fiction; it is historical fact, and, as such, is worthy of study; but, as Anatole France (1844-1924) pointed out:

The books that everybody admires are those that nobody reads.

How true that is of the Bible! Few actually read it, but even fewer study it. Why is this? When asked, many say that it is so hard to understand – even impossible – but isn't any textbook? How many people would understand a year eleven French book or a year nine Physics book if they had not been taught the content of the previous ones? In Acts 8:30-31 we read of the Ethiopian who was reading the prophecy of Isaiah; and, when asked if he understood what he was reading, he replied: "How can I, unless someone explains it to me?"

1 Corinthians 12 contains Paul's reprimand for misuse of the miraculous gifts of the Acts period. Ephesians 4:11 records people with other gifts– namely: apostles, prophets, evangelists, pastors, and teachers.

If Paul were alive today he would reprimand modern-day Christendom; for whereas many desire the offices of apostles and prophets, and great prestige is given to evangelists and pastors – who wants to be a teacher? Sadly there is a lack of good teachers of the Bible; and nowadays, when so few people know anything about the Bible, such a job is made even more difficult. The big problem is the initial study.

With the help of students in Queen Mary's Christian Union, I wrote the Manual on the Gospel of John. This publication teaches people about one of the most important books of the Bible; but it requires no previous knowledge of the Bible. Our desire was that it would help to get people started, and the question/answer format of it seems to have ensured success.

In conclusion:
The most important historical event

"Do not be afraid, for I know that you are looking for Jesus, who was crucified. He is not here; he has risen, just as he said. Come and see the place where he lay. Then go quickly and tell his disciples: 'He has risen from the dead and is going ahead of you into Galilee. There you will see him.' Now I have told you."

So the women hurried away from the tomb, afraid yet filled with joy, and ran to tell his disciples. Suddenly Jesus met them. "Greetings," he said. They came to him, clasped his feet and worshipped him. (Matthew 28:5-9)

Christ died for our sins according to the Scriptures ... he was buried ... he was raised on the third day, according to the Scriptures, and ... he appeared to Peter, and then to the Twelve. After that, he appeared to more than five hundred of the brothers at the same time, most of whom are still living, though some have fallen asleep. Then he appeared to James, then to all the apostles, and last of all he appeared to me also. (1 Corinthians 15:3-8)

The Corinthians were doubting the resurrection, and Paul was, in effect, telling them to go up to Jerusalem and talk to the eye witnesses.

However, are there any records, outside of the Bible, to the existence of Christ and of this great event, the resurrection of Jesus from the dead? I have listed many in a study called *The Existence of Christ*, which is freely available as a download from **www.obt.org.uk** which is the website of the Open Bible Trust. However, to quote but one of these records:

And there arose about this time Jesus, a wise man, if indeed we should call him a man: for he was a doer of marvellous deeds, a teacher of men who receive the truth with pleasure. He led away many of the Jews, and also many of the Greeks. This man was the Christ. And when Pilate had condemned him to the cross on his impeachment by the chief men among us, those who had loved him at first did not forsake him; for he appeared to them on the third day alive again, the divine prophets having spoken these and thousands of other wonderful things about him: and even now the tribe of Christians, so named after him, has not yet died out.

So wrote the non-Christian Josephus in Antiquities 18, 3, 3. However, some scholars have tried to cast doubt upon this statement by stating that the reference to Christ's resurrection is a corruption of the text, and was added years later by Christians. The argument against such a suggestion is contained in detail in the paper mentioned above, The Existence of Christ. Suffice it to say here that there is no textual evidence for this view. All ancient manuscript copies of Josephus contain these words.

Final Questions

Does anyone still think the Bible not worth *studying*? Does anyone still think there is nothing we can learn from it? Does anyone still side with Bradlaugh, and say that the Book is not worth the trouble and expense of translating? There can only be one answer – **there is no one.**

Section 3:
The Bible!
An Inspired Book?
Is It Worth Believing?

Some men borrow books, some men steal books, and others beg presentation copies from the author.

(JAMES JEFFREY ROCHE, 1847-1908)

There are seventy million books in American libraries, but the one you want to read is always out.

(TOM MASSON 1866-1934)

And many other signs truly did Jesus in the presence of his disciples, which are not written in this book; But these are written, that ye might believe that Jesus is the Christ, the Son of God; and that believing ye might have life through his name.

(JOHN 20:30-31, KJV)

If good books did good, the world would have been converted long ago.

(GEORGE MOORE, 1852-1933)

What is an Idiot?

Some years ago, when lecturing in mathematics at a college, I overheard some students talking as I was getting a coffee in the restaurant. They were not talking about me personally, but they basically said that someone like me was an idiot.

There are, as far as I know, three definitions of an idiot. For those who like to play around with I.Q. tests, an idiot can be defined as anyone who has an I.Q. below 70. At university mine was 140 plus and the last time I did an I.Q. test it was 135, and I suspect it has slipped further by now, but not below 70. So I can't be defined as an idiot on that score.

Then there is the dictionary definition of an idiot. I quote from *The Oxford Dictionary:*

> IDIOT – person so deficient in mind as to be permanently incapable of rational conduct and having a mental development not exceeding that of an average child of two years old.

Now, I am willing to concede that at times I am 'capable of irrational conduct'. For example when England beat Wales at Rugby, but I am not permanently incapable of such behaviour, so . . . I cannot be classified as an idiot by this definition.

The definition of 'idiot' which I heard that day, and since then in a variety of places, takes the form 'anyone who believes in the Bible is an idiot!' If that is a legitimate definition, then I am an idiot.

So far I have attempted to show that the Bible is a special book, worth reading, and a reliable book, worth studying. But is it more than that? Is it an inspired book, worth believing?

So, as a plea for my sanity, I would like to point out just a few things which made me stop and think about the Bible, and stopped me being sceptical about that book. These made me begin to wonder if that book was more than the work of mere men.

The world hangs on nothing

Let's start off by considering some of the earliest writings of the Bible. Job was possibly one of the first books to be written. It goes back over 3,500 years and in it we read:

> He [God] stretcheth out the north over the empty place, *and* hangeth the earth upon nothing. (Job 26:7 *KJV*)
> He suspends the earth over nothing. (Job 26:7, *NIV*)

Hangs the earth upon nothing? Suspends the earth over nothing? We can so easily read over that verse and accept it as nothing out of the ordinary because we know from modern science that the earth is suspended in space. But how did Job know it was true? That verse was written over 3,500 years ago. Job couldn't have known that the earth hangs upon nothing unless ... he was inspired by God!

The Greeks, a thousand years after Job, thought that the earth was supported on pillars set up by Hercules, but they never explained what supported the pillars. Similarly, in ancient India the view was that the earth was carried on the back of an elephant which stood on the back of a turtle ... But what did the turtle stand on? They didn't say, and yet, years before, Job had declared "he hangeth the world upon nothing". How absurd that statement must have appeared over the centuries! Thinking men, scientists and mathematicians must have ridiculed it for being obviously impossible and plainly stupid. But it was true. *We* know it was true, but how did Job know?

The seed of the woman

Probably the next writings were those attributed to Moses who wrote most of the first five books of the Old Testament about 3,500 years ago. In the first of those books we read:

> "And I will put enmity between thee and the woman, and between thy seed and her seed; ..." (Genesis 3:15, *KJV*; {margin *NIV*})

Her seed? The seed of woman? Well, we have all had to do biology at school and have studied such controversial subjects as the reproduction of the amoeba and hydra and how the birds and bees help in the pollination of plants. We all know how human reproduction works, so we read that verse and no one bats an eyelid at the expression 'her seed'. The reference to the seed of the woman causes no concern, yet until about a hundred years ago this was another controversial passage and open to ridicule. Up to that time, and certainly during Moses' time and for centuries afterwards, the idea was that the male, alone, produced the seed, and the woman was merely the garden in which that seed would grow. That tiny, microscopic egg, produced singly each month, was not detected until last century, thanks to microscopes. So, how did the writer of Genesis know about it? How did Moses, and the other writers in the Bible who refer to the seed of the woman, know? They must have acquired the knowledge from a source higher than mankind, from the Creator who knew how his creatures worked.

The number of stars

We pass over many interesting books and come to the prophet Jeremiah, who wrote in about 500 BC, i.e. about 2,500 years ago. In one verse he uses the expression:

> Countless as the stars of the sky. (Jeremiah 33:22, *NIV*)

However, about 1,000 years earlier than this we read in Genesis 15:5, where God told Abram:

> "Look up at the heavens and count the stars – if indeed you can count them." Then he said to him, "So shall your offspring be."

Now if these words, when they were first written, were thought to be a joke verse, we shouldn't be surprised. In 130 BC, about four hundred years later than Jeremiah, and many, many years after Abraham, the Greek astronomer and mathematician Hipparchus counted the stars in the sky and made the number 850. The case against Jeremiah's statement was strengthened by another astronomer and mathematician Ptolemy, a

Roman citizen of Egypt. In about AD 150 he made the number of stars 1022! Maybe some new ones had appeared, maybe it was a clear night, and maybe it was because the night sky was viewed from a different part of the earth or at a different time of the year. Anyway, 'the stars of heaven cannot be numbered' appeared to be untrue.

Untrue, that is, until some 350 years ago when Galileo took a look at the night sky through a telescope and found quite a few more! We, today, know that what Jeremiah said is true, that 'the stars of heaven cannot be numbered'. New ones appear in the telescopes, and others burn out. There are millions of them, billions of them; we cannot number them. We know this but how did Jeremiah know it?

But this verse in Jeremiah contains another thought!

> I will make the descendants of David my servant ... as countless as the stars of the sky and as measureless as the sand on the seashore. (Jeremiah 33:22)

This thought occurs over and over again throughout the Old Testament. Just as the stars cannot be numbered, just as the sand on the seashore cannot be measured, so will be the Jewish people. Again you can see how this verse was open to ridicule in Jeremiah's day. The 'official' figure for the number of stars was about 850; the 'official' figure for the number of Jews was a hundred times larger, at least. But, is it true that the Jewish people cannot be numbered? Has that statement of Jeremiah's come true? Who, today, can count the number of Jews scattered throughout the world? It's impossible. It wasn't like that in Jeremiah's day, when all the genealogies and records were kept in the Temple at Jerusalem. Why did he write it? How did he know it would become impossible to number the Jews? The great nation of Egypt with her Pharaohs has gone ... yet it had a much greater population than the Jewish nation. The great kingdom of Babylon with her King Nebuchadnezzar, gone, but again ... it was much greater in population. Gone is the colossal Roman Empire. But the persecuted Jews struggle on and produce children to overcome the loss of millions put to death. How do they manage to survive? You would never have thought that such a nation could outlive the mighty nations of Egypt, Babylon and Rome ... and yet Jeremiah states:

> This is what the Lord says,
>> he who appoints the sun to shine by day,
>> who decrees the moon and stars to shine by night, who stirs up the sea so that its waves roar-the Lord Almighty is his name:
> "Only if these decrees vanish from my sight," declares the Lord,
> "Will the descendants of Israel ever cease to be a nation before me."
> (Jeremiah 31:35-36)

Is that the reason this nation has been able to overcome all the persecution it has received? Behind the scenes of physical reality, God is protecting them? Is that the reason? What other explanation is there?

Let us look at these verses from another angle. How true they are! We know that if the sun and moon depart then not only would the people of Israel depart, but so too would the whole world population. Did Jeremiah know that? Maybe, maybe not, but look at the next verse.

> "Only if the heavens above can be measured and the foundations of the earth below be searched out will I reject all the descendants of Israel because of all they have done." (Jeremiah 31:37)

We know that the foundations of the earth cannot be searched out, for below the surface is the hot, molten outer core. Yet some of the Greeks of Jeremiah's time, and after, believed in Hades, the underworld.

What about the heavens? Do we take the Big Bang theory or the Steady State theory? Is the universe expanding or in a state of oscillation? Whichever the theory, whatever the state, we in this generation can appreciate, even if we cannot comprehend, the vastness of the heavens. We can appreciate the vastness of the universe far, far more than generation before us. How true are Jeremiah's words, "the heavens above cannot be measured"; but how did Jeremiah come to such great understanding? His explanation is found in verse 35:

This is what the Lord says.

Do we accept his explanation or do we reject it? If we reject it, we ought to have a *viable* alternative explanation.

So we see that the continuous existence of the Jewish people is assured. God has promised to protect them, but he has also promised to discipline them. Through Jeremiah we learn that, if they disobeyed God and failed to worship him, they would be dispersed among the nations of the world (see Jeremiah 9:16 and 13:24). But the Bible also states (e.g. in Ezekiel 11:17) that after a time they would be gathered from those nations and restored and their land in the Middle East.

Now, many commentators think that such promises were fulfilled not long after they were written. The Jewish nation was exiled to Babylon and did return after seventy years to rebuild Jerusalem. However, that nation's rejection of Christ, and refusal to repent at Peter's calling (Acts 3:19-21), saw another period of disobedience which resulted in the Romans scattering them throughout the whole world after AD 70.

They remained homeless, not for seventy years but for centuries. That is, until 1948, when the Jewish state was set up in Palestine, that self-same Middle Eastern land. In 1967 the Jews acquired more land and the whole of Jerusalem, and 1974 saw further expansion. Are we seeing biblical prophecy being fulfilled before our very eyes? I don't know, but keep your eyes on the news from that part of the world. Parts of the Bible indicate that the ancient Temple, destroyed by the Romans when they invaded in AD 70, will be rebuilt.

We are living in exciting times. But how did people such as Jeremiah and Ezekiel know about such things thousands of years before they happened? This makes you think, and can you dismiss it? I can't.

All humanity destroyed

Let's look at one more prophecy. When writing about the return of Christ, Matthew states that unless that event happened, i.e. unless those days were cut short, "... there should no flesh be saved; ..." (*KJV*). i.e. "no one would survive" (*NIV*). Matthew 24:22).

Now, many scoff at the idea of God, in the person of Christ, intervening in the daily life and events of this world, but do we scoff at the idea of humanity destroying itself? That was not possible until the last century, but now we know that man has enough nuclear warheads to destroy this planet not once not twice, but maybe half-a-dozen times; and some people are gravely concerned about chemical and germ warfare, and weapons of mass-destruction.

People have asked, what right has God got to intervene in the life of this planet? Every right, when the creature he has made is about to destroy himself totally. Thus, to stop mankind committing such folly, the Bible states that Christ will return to this earth ... and do you know where?

> On that day his feet will stand on the Mount of Olives, east of Jerusalem, and the Mount of Olives will be split in two from east to west, forming a great valley, with half of the mountain moving north and half moving south. (Zechariah 14:4)

So ... the return of Christ to the Mount of Olives is an event which is to be accompanied by a great earthquake. Do you realize that geologists have discovered a fault line running east-west, right through the middle of that mountain? One day there will be a devastating earthquake there. But how did Zechariah know about it? Had he a seismograph? No. There was no way he could have known ... unless it was revealed to him from above.

What was inspired?

Until about 600 years ago there was no version of the Bible in the English language. The Bible mainly used in Britain was in Latin, and the chief reason for learning that language was to be able to read the Bible.

Before AD 735, Bede had made an Anglo-Saxon translation of John's Gospel, and in the next century King Alfred did the same for the Psalms.

In the 10th century the Latin text of the Lindisfarne Gospels was interlined with an Old English paraphrase; i.e. Old English words were inserted between the lines of Latin text. However, few of the population could read. The main motive for learning to read was to be able to read those passages of the Bible.

John Wycliffe produced the first English version in 1384; but this was not freely available, and anyway, the vast majority of the population still couldn't read. In 1454 the printing press was invented, and in 1525 William Tyndale produced the first *printed* New Testament in English. This momentous event was quickly surpassed by Miles Coverdale[6] who, in 1535, produced the first printed English version of the whole Bible. This was followed in 1539 by the Great Bible. But all these were large, unwieldy volumes, not readily available to those members of the public who could read.

In the 16th century, Roman type-face was developed for the printing press and replaced the Gothic 'black letters'. This enabled books to be produced in a smaller size; and, at the same time, made them easier to read. In 1560 the Geneva Bible was produced, the first of all the small-print Bibles.

Eight years later the English bishops got together, produced their own translation and printed that. All the New Testament versions that followed Tyndale's of 1525 were based on his translation. There were many English versions around, but most were translated from the Latin and took little notice of the original Greek. These different translations vied with one another for acceptance, but none seemed to stand out significantly above the rest. Then King James I authorized scholars to make a translation of the Bible direct from the original Hebrew and Greek. This King James Version (*KJV*) appeared in 1611 and was accepted as the 'Authorized Version', the one with authority. Slowly the other translations mentioned above fell into disuse.

---

[6] For more on Miles Coverdale see Michael Penny's *Approaching the Bible* (see page 175) which is based upon words from the introduction to Coverdale's Bible, and with an appendix dedicated to Coverdale.

The New Testament of the King James Version was translated mainly from a Greek text known as the *Textus Receptus* (or Received Text) which had been constructed by Erasmus in Holland in 1516. The Old Testament was based on the 10th century Massoretic Hebrew text. But over the next couple of hundred years many more ancient biblical texts, and non-biblical texts in Hebrew and Greek, were discovered. It was in the light of such discoveries that the revisers of the King James Version produced the Revised Version between 1881 and 1885, for the New and Old Testaments, respectively.

Since that time many more manuscripts have come to light, and there is now quite a variety of New Testament texts. Most modern translations of the Bible have not relied upon a single text but have constructed their own eclectic one; i.e. they have used all available material and, following the principles of textual criticism, they weigh up the different manuscripts and take from the one which for them gives the most authoritative reading for that particular word, verse, passage or chapter.

How the Bible came to us

	Old Testament in Hebrew and Chaldee (Aramaic). Scribes made copies on scrolls.
	The First Translation of the Hebrew OT into Greek; known as The Septuagint (LXX). Made in the 3rd Century BC by 72 Jews.
1st century AD The writings of people such as Paul, John, Peter, James and others spread throughout the Roman Empire, and were eventually brought together as the Bible.	New Testament in Greek. Single pages of papyrus or vellum used and bound as a book.
4th to 6th centuries. The first Christian missionaries came to Britain, bringing the Bible in Latin.	Latin translations
	Jerome (died c 405) revised the Latin versions using Greek and Hebrew Texts
6th century onwards Latin manuscripts were copied and illuminated by monks	Lindisfarne Gospels, illuminated Latin manuscripts of the four Gospels
	Bede (died 735). Anglo-Saxon version of John's Gospel
	King Alfred (died 899). Anglo-Saxon version of the Psalms.
10th century	10th Century. Lindisfarne Gospels, interlined with an Old English paraphrase
12th to 15th centuries In churches and cathedrals biblical truths were conveyed in stained glass windows, paintings and sculptures. Mass of the population was illiterate	John Wycliffe. First English Bible, 1384.

15th Century 1440 the invention of the printing press in Europe led to a great increase in the production of books. In 1453, scholars fleeing to the west from Constantinople, bring with them the Greek text of the Bible.	William Tyndale. First printed English New Testament, 1525
	Miles Coverdale. First printed English Bible, 1535
	The Great Bible Coverdale's English version, 1539; also the revisions, especially by Cranmer in 1540
16th century Typeface was developed and replaced 'black letter', making it possible to produce books of smaller size yet easier to read. Bibles were set up in churches and, by the time of Elizabeth I, took their place in English homes	The Geneva Bible. First small print English Bible, in Roman type, 1560
	The Bishop's Bible. English translation prepared by the bishops, 1568
17th century King James I commissioned scholars to translate the Bible into English from Hebrew and Greek	The King James Authorised Version (*KJV*) English translation from the Hebrew and Greek, 1611
19th century The Industrial Revolution produced even better printing machines to enable the demand for popular education to be met. Societies were formed to encourage the spread of the Bible.	The Revised Version (*RV*) A Revision of the King James Version, 1881-85
20th century Many new translations were made.	Some other English translations: 1901 American Standard Version (*ASV*) 1952 Revised Standard Version 1966 Jerusalem Bible 1970 New English Bible (*NEB*) 1976 Good News Bible (*GNB*) 1978 New International Version (*NIV*) 1982 New King James Version (*NKJV*)

So ... what is inspired? I do not believe that any English Bible is inspired. The majority of those who believe the Bible to be the inspired Word of God, believe that the *original* writings themselves were given by God. After that man became responsible for the preservation and safe-keeping, as soon as they were committed to paper. This would certainly be in harmony with the views of the Jews. We saw in chapter 2 above the trouble they took in endeavouring to make an error-free copy. They believed they were handling the Word of God, and they knew that they were responsible for preserving it and for guarding it against error.

This view would also be in harmony with that of such people as the apostles Paul and Peter. Paul wrote:

"All Scripture *is* given by inspiration of God ..." [or is 'God-breathed']. (2 Timothy 3:16; *KJV*)

Peter wrote:

For prophecy never had its origin in the will of man, but men spoke from God as they were carried along by the Holy Spirit. (2 Peter 1:21)

There is no doubt that Peter and Paul were thinking primarily of the Jewish Scriptures, the Old Testament; but neither is there any doubt that they considered the New Testament writings to be of equal standing, and to have the same origin. For example, Peter wrote:

Bear in mind that our Lord's patience means salvation, just as our dear brother *Paul also wrote to you with the wisdom that God gave him.* He writes the same way in all his letters, speaking in them of these matters. His letters contain some things that are hard to understand, which ignorant and unstable people distort, *as they do the other Scripture.* (2 Peter 3:15-16)

Paul's letters were being distorted, as were the OTHER Scriptures. Thus Peter considered Paul's writing to be Scripture, to be of equal standing as the Old Testament, to have the same origin, and to be inspired. Was Paul aware of this? He wrote:

And we also thank God continually because, *when you received the Word of God, which you heard from us, you accepted it not as the word of men, but as it actually is, the Word of God.* (1 Thessalonians 2:13)

We may be wondering how people such as Peter and Paul, and especially the writers of the Gospels, could get things correct, writing so many years after the events. Speaking to the Twelve, the Lord Jesus Christ told them:

> But the Counsellor, the Holy Spirit, whom the Father will send in my name, will teach you all things and *will remind you of everything I have said to you.* (John 14:26)

The Holy Spirit "he shall teach you all things" and will "bring all things to your remembrance, whatsoever I have said unto you" (*KJV*). Thus writers like Matthew and John could remember, years later, the exact words the Lord Jesus Christ had said – thanks to the Holy Spirit. Thus God breathed, and the writers were carried along by that breath, by the Holy Spirit. They remembered accurately, and the Holy Spirit taught them, and so the inspired Scriptures were recorded. But once written down ... what happened to them then?

We saw in Chapter 2 the incredible trouble taken by the Jews to ensure they got an accurate and correct copy of any particular book of the Scriptures. From this alone it is evident that they did not consider any copyist to be "carried along by the Holy Spirit", as was the original writer. The copyist would pray and seek strength to perform his task, but he was not inspired. An accurate copy of the original inspired writings was man's responsibility. They were aware of that, so set up the elaborate system for copying, and the detailed Massorah for checking.

Evidence and Assessment: Objective not Subjective

SUBJECTIVE – Arising from the senses; relating to, or affecting, thoughts and feelings of the person; imaginary, illusory; of, proceeding from within.

OBJECTIVE – Relating to that which is external to the mind; exhibiting actual facts unclouded by the exhibitor's feelings; dealing with actual things and not with thoughts, feelings or opinions.

Some have pointed to 2 Peter 3:10:

> But the day of the Lord will come like a thief.
>> The heavens will disappear with a roar;
> the elements will be destroyed by fire,
>> and the earth and everything in it will be laid bare.

Some have suggested that this could support the inspiration of Scripture because only in the last century has man discovered how to melt the chemical elements. However, the word used by Peter and translated elements may not mean chemical elements, the definition of which did not arise till centuries after Peter wrote those words. The original word could mean the physical elements of the earth – such as wood, clay, rock, water, etc. Even with that definition, 2 Peter 3:10 is significant.

Again some have pointed to Zechariah who also spoke about the still future day of the Lord:

> This is the plague with which the Lord will strike all the nations that fought against Jerusalem: Their flesh will rot while they are still standing on their feet their eyes will rot in their sockets, and their tongues will rot in their mouths. (Zechariah 14:12)

This, some suggest, could be the result of radio-active fall-out and thus another good verse to support the inspiration of Scripture. This may have some validity. True! Zechariah could never have seen such a plague, but can we be dogmatic and state that it must be the result of radio-active fall-out? It could be the result of germ or chemical warfare.

In the presentation and appraisal of evidence, believers and unbelievers must attempt to be objective. It is so easy for supporters of the Bible to supply subjective evidence, to read into passages something which isn't there. Similarly it is so easy for the opponents of the Bible to be subjective about their evidence and to refuse to accept something which is obvious. Both supporter and opponent must attempt to be objective. We stress attempt because it is probably impossible for anyone to be 100 per cent objective. We are all tied up with ourselves, our own lives, our own thoughts and experiences, but we must make a valiant attempt to be impartial. Objective evidence and objective assessment are so crucial. We must try and deal with facts and not with thoughts, feelings and senses. We can profitably discuss facts, and if we differ over the interpretation of them we can respectfully disagree with one another; but it is much more difficult to disagree amicably over thoughts, feelings and senses.

"He ... hangeth the earth upon nothing" (Job 26:7, KJV) is a plain statement. The comments made about it earlier were objectively presented and an unbiased appraisal of those comments can produce only one response – how did Job know?

Similarly the comments about the seed of woman in Genesis 3:15. Similarly Jeremiah's statements about the stars being uncountable, and about it being impossible to measure the heavens above and search out the earth beneath. In these there has been an attempt to be 100 per cent objective by presenting *facts* and by presenting them fairly and squarely and not emotionally.

Facts, such as the future earthquake that will split the Mount of Olives, written about in Zechariah, and the ability of man to destroy himself, recorded in Matthew ... in all these the aim has been to get the factual evidence and to present it impartially. We can but hope that those who read this book will attempt to do likewise; but to be totally dispassionate is very difficult, almost impossible. It is hard for any of us to stand outside our preconceived ideas, with their built-in biases; but to be aware of them is the first step.

Some would claim that the most dominant force in man is his emotion, and at times many have been overcome with joy or sorrow, happiness or grief, love or (unfortunately) hate. During such times it is almost, if not absolutely, impossible to think clearly, logically and unemotionally. Many writers and orators have played on the emotions of their readers and listeners, and the results can be staggering. The case seems so powerful and the evidence so overwhelming, but ... does the effect last? In the cold light of morning, some days, weeks or months afterwards, that reader, that listener, is left with nothing. The emotion has gone and he returns to his former habits, his former views, his former beliefs. An attempt to present evidence objectively is far less spectacular and may well win fewer (initial) converts; but those gained by this method are far less likely to go back on it. Thus we shall endeavour to present objective evidence objectively and ask our readers to attempt to display a similar attitude in their assessment of it.

Points to be considered

I have attempted to supply objective evidence, and whether this presentation was impartial and unemotional, the reader can judge for himself. The evidence fell into two categories.

- Passages of the Bible which recorded what we today know as facts – but which couldn't have been known at the time, unless revealed by a higher source.
- Passages of the Bible which said what would happen in the future; i.e. prophecy.

We shall look at both of these in more detail, and also consider other evidence.

Point 1 – Facts recorded before they were known

We have mentioned several of these already in this chapter, but present them here in a list.

(1) Hanging the world *on* nothing (Job 26:7)
(2) The seed of woman (Genesis 3:15)
(3) The stars cannot be numbered (Jeremiah 33:22)
(4) The Jews cannot be numbered (Genesis 13:16; 15:5; Jeremiah 33:22)
(5) The heavens cannot be measured (Jeremiah 31:37)
(6) The earth beneath cannot be searched out (Jeremiah 31:37)
(7) Humanity can destroy itself (Matthew 24:22)
(8) The fault line through the Mount of Olives (Zechariah 14:4)

(9) The plague that rots the body (Zechariah 14:12)

We would urge our reader to study the Bible, attempting to put themselves into the time (and with the knowledge) of the writer. Doing that will bring to light many other items which could be added to the above list. It will also increase one's understanding and appreciation of the passage. We add some more from the book of Genesis.

(10) Genesis 1:9. The waters gathered together in one place, and the land gathered together in one place. Assuming the Continental Drift theory is correct, it is now though that all the land was, at one time, in one place. However, there is no way the writer of Genesis could have known that.

(11) Genesis 1:1-31. These verses give the order in which life appeared on earth. Modern-day biologists know that this is the correct and necessary order. Was Moses a biologist? No, he was educated in the schools of Egypt which taught that all life came from the mud of the river Nile. Moses obviously did not go along with the thinking of his day. What changed his mind? Or who?

(12) Genesis 7:19 records that the whole world was covered by the flood. There was no way Noah or Moses could have known the extent of that flood, yet archaeological evidence would indicate that this was so.

The Jews of Berea (Acts 17:10-11) searched the Scriptures to see for themselves. We ask the reader to do the same and to discover some more fascinating facts: facts recorded but which could not have been known by the authors – unless they were supplied 'from above'.

Point 2 – The testimony of prophecy

We mentioned earlier how difficult or even impossible it is to be 100 per cent objective. It is so easy to let personal, inward views cloud our thoughts and distort the evidence one way or the other. No subject suffers from this more than biblical prophecy. Christ's words in Matthew 24:6-7 give us a classic example.

"You will hear of wars and rumours of wars, but see to it that you are not alarmed. Such things must happen but the end is still to come.

Nation will rise against nation, and kingdom against kingdom. There will be famines and earthquakes in various places."

Here, some say, is a prophecy that predicts that throughout the course of time there will be war after war. Nation will rise against nation and kingdom against kingdom and there will be earth-quakes and subsequent famines. This, some say, shows that Christ was more than a mere man and the Bible more than a mere book – but is that view tenable? An objective assessment of those verses in Matthew, together with *that* interpretation, would result in the view that Christ was a very wise man who understood human nature, as well as politics, and that Matthew had recorded his words more or less correctly. Here some Christians have allowed their desire to support their Lord and the Bible to cloud their understanding of the passage. If we attempt to look at the passage objectively, what do we get?

(1) Christ is answering a question posed by the disciples in Matthew 24:1-3. They wanted to know three things:
    (a) When would the Temple be destroyed?
    (b) What will be the sign of Christ's second coming?
    (c) What will be the sign of the end of the age?

(2) This whole passage is addressed to the people in Jerusalem and Judea (Matthew 24:16) and to those who will "hear of wars and rumours of wars"; or, as the *New English Bible* puts it:

"The time is coming when you will hear the noise of battle near at hand and the news of battles far away." (Matthew 24:6)

Thus, piecing together this prophecy, we see it is addressed to people in Jerusalem and Judea who, in days approaching the end of the age and preceding the return of Christ, are to hear the sound of wars and to receive the news of wars. But what wars will they receive news about?

(3) Some think "nation against nation" is alluding to 2 Chronicles 15:6 which refers to the nations around the land of Palestine. "Kingdom against kingdom" is a phrase that occurs in Isaiah 19:2 and some think

that the Lord Jesus is quoting from that passage, which also deals with the kingdoms around Palestine. So we see that the passage is saying that people in Judea, in the days leading up to the return of Christ at the end of the age, will hear the sound of war and will receive news of wars between the kingdoms and the nations that surround their country. Anyone who listens to the Middle East news should now sit up! An objective interpretation of this prophecy is startling. An objective assessment of it is staggering.

(4) But the prophecy goes on. In those days, also, there will be "famines and earthquakes in various places". There have always been earthquakes, so this might not appear much of a prophecy; but let us look back over the years of this century. (Earthquakes are measured on the Richter scale; the higher the number, the greater the earthquake.) The following is taken from Stan Deyo's *Cosmic Conspiracy:*

(a) Between the years 1897 and 1946, the average number of earthquakes above Richter 6 was 3 per decade; i.e. there were about 15 earthquakes over Richter 6 during those 50 years.
(b) Between 1947 and 1956 there were 7 earthquakes above Richter 6; i.e. there were 7 during those 10 years.
(c) Between 1957 and 1966 there were 17 earthquakes above Richter 6; i.e. there were 17 during those 10 years.
(d) In 1967, *alone* there were 17 earthquakes above Richter 6.
(e) In 1968 there were 19 earthquakes above Richter 6.
(f) In 1969 there were 21 above Richter 6.
(g) In 1970 there were 24 above Richter 6.
(h) In 1971 there were 34 above Richter 6.
(i) Between 1967 and 1976 there were over 180 earthquakes over Richter 7 (seven, not six!)

However, since then the number of earthquakes, and especially larger ones, has continued to increase. September 2010 saw the terrible earthquake in Christchurch, New Zealand, and March 2011 saw one of the largest earthquakes ever hit Japan.

The United States Geological Survey gives the following results for the start of the 21st century – a full table from 1970-2010 is given in Appendix 7.

year	number of earthquakes in magnitude range					estimated deaths
	8.0 to 9.9	7.0 to 7.9	6.0 to 6.9	5.0 to 5.9	5.0 to 9.9	
2000	1	14	146	1,344	1,505	231
2001	1	15	121	1,224	1,361	21,357
2002	0	13	127	1,201	1,341	1,685
2003	1	14	140	1,203	1,358	33,819
2004	2	14	141	1,515	1,672	228,802
2005	1	10	140	1,693	1,844	82,364
2006	2	9	142	1,712	1,865	6,605
2007	4	14	178	2,074	2,270	712
2008	0	12	168	1,768	1,948	88,011
2009	1	16	141	1,872	2,030	1,787
2010[7]	1	19	135	1,547	1,702	226,668

Associated with earthquakes are famines. Thus when we look dispassionately at Matthew 24:6-7, and look at it in the whole context, attempting to establish exactly what it means, the result is simply amazing. *The marvellous thing about biblical prophecy is the way in which exact details are given.* The reader can now appreciate the exact meaning of Matthew 24:6-7, and it is up to him to decide whether that prophecy is beginning to come true.

---

[7] Figures for 2010 are not for the full year. They are up to November 7th.

But which biblical prophecies have been fulfilled? To answer that question would require several books. Well ... how many have come true? Dozens and dozens ... and by 'come true' we mean that they have been fulfilled in their exact details. If we 'prophesied' that we would receive a letter within the next month, that would not be much of a prophecy. If we said we would have a letter on the 5th day of next month, that would be more specific, but if it were fulfilled it wouldn't be out of the ordinary. We would need to 'prophesy', for example, that on the 5th day of next month we would receive three letters: one from London, one from Birmingham and one from Leeds – and the one from Leeds would have no stamp on it and we would be required by the postman to pay the excess fee. That would be very specific, and, if it happened, it might not convince a biased observer that we had the 'gift of prophecy' but it might make him say, "Let me have another example! Let's have another prophecy fulfilled. If you can do something like that again then you will start to convince me."

The Bible is a big book and makes many prophetic statements, so that if one or two came true, no one should be surprised. If, however, a dozen or so are fulfilled, an unbiased observed should be provoked to ask how could such a thing be possible? When the number of fulfillments runs into dozens and dozens, there can only be one conclusion.

As so many biblical prophecies have come true, it is impossible to deal with them all. Which shall we select? The central character of the Bible is the Lord Jesus Christ and the paramount event of his life was his crucifixion and subsequent resurrection and ascension. Stuart Allen, in his book, *The Unfolding Purpose of God*, lists fourteen prophecies concerning Christ which all came true, literally and specifically, within a period of twenty-four hours. All the prophecies were written 500 to 1,500 years before that fateful day on which they happened. Let us look at them.

1.   The Lord's disciples were to forsake him

Prophecy: Zechariah 13:7	Fulfilment: Mark 14:27
'Awake, O sword, against my shepherd, against the man who is close to me!' declares the Lord...'Strike the shepherd, and the sheep will be scattered.'	'You will all fall away,' Jesus told them, 'for it is written: "I will strike the shepherd, and the sheep will be scattered."'

2.   He was to be dumb before his accusers

Prophecy: Isaiah 53:7	Fulfilment: Matthew 27:12-14
He was oppressed and afflicted, yet he did not open his mouth; he was led like a lamb to the slaughter, and as a sheep before her shearers is silent, so he did not open his mouth.	When he was accused by the chief priests and the elders, he gave no answer. Then Pilate asked him, 'Don't you hear how many things they are accusing you of?' But Jesus made no reply, not even to a single charge – to the great amazement of the governor.

3.   He was to be wounded and bruised

Prophecy: Isaiah 53:5	Fulfilment: Matthew 27:26, 30
But he was pierced for our transgressions, he was crushed for our iniquities; the punishment that brought us peace was upon him, and by his wounds we are healed.	But he [Pilate] had Jesus flogged, and handed him over to be crucified ... They spat upon him, and took the staff and struck him on the head again and again.

4.   His hands and feet were to be pierced

Prophecy: Psalm 22:16	Fulfilment: Luke 23:33
...a band of evil men has encircled me, they have pierced my hands and my feet.	When they came to the place called The Skull, there they crucified him.

5. Yet none of his bones would be broken

Prophecy: Exodus 12:46 It [the Passover lamb] must be eaten inside one house; ... Do not break any of the bones.'	*Fulfilment:* John 19:31-36 The Jews ... asked Pilate to have the legs broken ... The soldiers ...broke the legs of the first man who had been crucified with Jesus, and then those of the other. But when they came to Jesus and found that he was already dead, they did not break his legs. ... These things happened so that the Scripture would be fulfilled: 'Not one of his bones will be broken.'

6. He was crucified with thieves

Prophecy: Isaiah 53:12 He was numbered with the transgressors.	*Fulfilment:* Mark 15:27-28 (margin) They crucified two robbers with him and the Scripture was fulfilled which says, 'He was counted with the lawless ones.'

7. He was to pray for his persecutors

Prophecy: Isaiah 53:12 For he bore the sin of many, and made intercession for the transgressors.	*Fulfilment:* Luke 23:34 Jesus said, 'Father, forgive them, for they do not know what they are doing.'

8. The people were to ridicule him

Prophecy: Psalm 22:7-8 All who see me mock me; they hurl insults, shaking their heads. 'He trusts in the Lord; let the Lord rescue him. Let him deliver him, since he delights in him.'	*Fulfilment:* Matthew 27:41-43 The chief priests, the teachers of the law and the elders mocked him. 'He saved others' they said, 'but he can't save himself! He's the king of Israel! Let him come

	down now from the cross, and we will believe in him. He trusts in God. Let God rescue him now if he wants him.'

9. His garments were to be parted and lots cast for his vesture

Prophecy: Psalm 22:18	Fulfilment: John 19:23-24
They divide my garments among them and cast lots for my clothing.	They took his clothes, dividing them into four shares, one for each of them, with the undergarment remaining ... 'Let's not tear it,' they said to one another. 'Let's decide by lot who will get it.' This happened that the Scripture might be fulfilled which said, 'They ... cast lots for my clothing.'

10. The cry from the cross

Prophecy: Psalm 22:1	Fulfilment: Matthew 27:46
'My God, my God, why have you forsake me?'	About the ninth hour Jesus cried out in a loud voice, 'Eloi, Eloi, lama sabachthani?' – which means, 'My God, my God, why have you forsaken me?'

11. They were to give him gall and vinegar to drin

Prophecy: Psalm 69:21	Fulfilment: Matthew 27:34
They put gall in my food and gave me vinegar for my thirst.	There they offered him wine to drink, mixed with gall; but after tasting it, he refused to drink it.

12. His body was to be pierced'

Prophecy: Zechariah 12:10	Fulfilment: John 19:34-37
'They [Israel] will look on me [the Lord, verse 8], the one they have pierced, and mourn for him ...'	One of the soldiers pierced Jesus' side with a spear, bringing a sudden flow of blood and water. The man who saw it has given testimony, and his testimony is true. He knows that he tells the truth, and he testifies so that you also may believe. These things happened so that the Scripture would be fulfilled: 'Not one of his bones will be broken,' and, as another Scripture says, 'They will look on the one they have pierced.'

13. His heart was to be broken

Prophecy: Psalm 22:14	Fulfilment: John 19:34
I am poured out like water, and all my bones are out of joint. My heart has turned to wax; it has melted away within me.	One of the soldiers pierced Jesus' side ... bringing a sudden flow of blood and water.

14. He was buried in a rich man's grave

Prophecy: Isaiah 53:9	Fulfilment: Matthew 27:57-60
He was assigned a grave with the wicked [plural], and with the rich [singular] in his death.	As evening approached, there came a rich man from Arimathea, name Joseph ... going to Pilate, he asked for Jesus' body ... Joseph took the body, wrapped it in clean linen cloth, and placed it in his own new tomb that he had cut out of the rock.

We can but repeat, all these events were prophesied some 500 to 1,500 years before they occurred, and note...they all happened exactly as had been predicted. They were *all* fulfilled *literally* and not in any figurative, allegorical, spiritual or mystical way.

What can we say? There are some who will take the view that the second prophecy (He was dumb before his accusers) is not really a prophecy. They would claim that Christ undoubtedly knew that passage of Isaiah and so kept silent to make it happen. Similarly with the seventh (He was to pray for his accusers); here, some claim, Christ in agony on the cross remembered Isaiah 53:12. Again the tenth (The cry from the cross); here, in intense pain, Christ remembered Psalm 22:1. These may be fair comments, the reader can judge for himself, but the fact is there are still eleven other prophecies to be faced.

- Did Jesus purposely make his disciples forsake him?
- Did he purposely go out of his way to make the soldiers bruise him?
- Did he purposely get the people to ridicule him?

Surely the answer to all these questions is 'No!' But anyway, what about the other prophecies listed above? From a human standpoint...

- He had no control over the fact that the soldiers did not break his legs.
- He had no control over the fact that he was crucified with thieves.
- He had no control over the fact that his garments were to be parted and lots cast for his vesture.
- He had no control over what they gave him to drink.
- He had no control over the fact that they decided to pierce his side with a sword.
- He had no control over where he was buried.

So, how can these specific prophecies be explained, other than by the fact that the writers were inspired by God? Some would say 'by chance', but that view is unreasonable. One lucky guess may come right, literally and specifically on a certain day. Two lucky guesses might...but three? That's beginning to push things. But here we don't have one or two or three. Here we have fourteen!

Let us say that a lucky guess has a 1 in 10 chance of coming right on any one day.

Two such lucky guesses have a 1 in 100 chance (10 x 10 = 100) of coming right, together, on the same day.

Three such lucky guesses have a one in 1,000 chance of coming right, together, on the same day. (10 x 10 x10 = 1,000.)

But how about fourteen lucky guesses? Fourteen lucky guesses have a 1 in 100,000,000,000,000 chance of coming right, together, on the same day. (That is 10 multiplied by itself 13 times. That figure is a hundred British billions or a hundred thousand American billions!)

We could go on and give much more evidence from this interesting and fascinating field of prophecy. However, sufficient has been given to convince the reader of the value of prophecy in showing the Bible to be God's inspired Word.

There are over sixty Old Testament prophecies fulfilled by the Lord Jesus Christ (these are listed in Appendix 4); and there are many, many others that do not relate directly to him, which have also come true. There are still many prophecies, as yet unfulfilled, but what can we say? The Bible student who has seen so many come true is convinced that prophecies such as the one about the great earthquake splitting the Mount of Olives, and its related events, *will* come true...and it may not be that far in the future!

Point 3 – The testimony of probability

In the previous section we touched a little on probability. It may have been difficult for some of our readers to follow, and to these we apologize. Mathematics, numbers and probability have often caused people problems, yet none would doubt their value in practically every walk of life.

There are books which use probability to show that the Bible is God's inspired word, and we give one detailed example. Will the probability turn out to be less than 1 in 100, or 1 in 1000? If it does then we should consider it to be unusual, out of the ordinary. Consider Leviticus 26:31-33,

(1) I will turn your cities into ruins and lay waste your sanctuaries, and
(2) I will take no delight in the pleasing aroma of your offerings.
(3) I will lay waste the land, so that your enemies who live there shall
    be appalled.
(4) I will scatter you among the nations and
(5) will draw out my sword and pursue you.
(6) Your land will be laid waste, and your cities will lie in ruins.

Here we have six predictions:
(1) The cities of Palestine will become ruins.
(2) The sanctuaries will be laid waste.
(3) The land will be laid waste.
(4) Enemies will live in that land.
(5) The people of Israel will be scattered.
(6) The people of Israel will be persecuted by the sword and pursued.

In his book *Science Speaks: An Evaluation of Certain Christian Evidences,* Peter Stoner suggests that the probability of each of these events is as follows:
(1) 1 in 10 for the cities becoming ruins.
(2) 1 in 2 for the sanctuaries being laid waste.
(3) 1 in 10 for the land being laid waste.
(4) 1 in 2 for enemies inhabiting the land.
(5) 1 in 5 for the people being scattered.
(6) 1 in 10 for the people being persecuted.

What is the probability of all six events happening? The answer is:

$$\frac{1}{10} \times \frac{1}{2} \times \frac{1}{10} \times \frac{1}{2} \times \frac{1}{5} \times \frac{1}{10} = \frac{1}{20,000}$$

That is 1 in 20,000, much more significant than 1 in 100 or 1 in 1000, but ... has it happened? Leviticus was written about BC and most commentators agree that the prophecy came true from AD 70 onwards, when the Romans scattered the Jews over the empire. Werner Keller's *The Bible as History* tells us:

> Archaeologists have found no material evidence of Israel's existence in Palestine [roughly present-day Israel, the Gaza strip and the West Bank] after the year 70 [AD], not even a tombstone with a Jewish inscription. The synagogues were destroyed; even the house of God in quiet Capernaum was reduced to ruins.

So this 1 in 20,000 chance happened! Isn't that enough to show that behind the writers of the Bible was an unseen hand?

If the above doesn't convince the reader we mention the prophecy concerning Tyre given in Ezekiel 26:3-21. Peter Stoner works out the probability of that prophecy's coming true as 1 in 75 million. Much more significant than the 1 in 100 which would make a statistician think an event unusual and out of the ordinary.

We say no more. Interested readers can obtain Peter Stoner's book for themselves. We are aware that the above will convince the already converted and cause them to rejoice, but what about those who are sceptical about the divine origin of the Scriptures? We would just ask them to remember that a statistician would start to question at a probability of 5 in 100. When it drops to below 1 in 100 he would start to look for explanations other than 'by chance'. At 1 in 20,000, at 1 in a million, at 1 in 75 million...surely there can be no doubt.

Point 4 – The testimony of numerics

In today's society we use Arabic numerals, i.e. 1, 2, 3, 4, 5, 6, 7, 8, 9. 0. By combining these in various ways we can represent the number we want; e.g. 31; 365; 2,600.

The Romans did not have these but used instead, certain letters of their alphabet to represent numbers, e.g. I = 1; V = 5; X = 10; L = 50; C = 100; D = 500; M = 1,000. By combining these they could represent the number they required, e.g. XIV = 14; CCCLXV = 365.

But how did the Greeks and Hebrews represent numbers? They used all the letters of their own alphabet, plus a few extra symbols, as follows:

The Hebrew Alphabet consists of 22 (2 x 11) letters. However, 5 extra symbols, called finals, were added (for 500, 600, 700, 800 and 900) to make up three series of 9, or 27 in all:

Aleph 1	1=א	Yod	י=10	Koph	ק=100
Beth	ב=2	Kaph	כ=20	Resh	ר=200
Gimel	ג=3	Lamed	ל=30	Shin	ש=300
Daleth	ד=4	Mem	מ=40	Tau	ת=400
He	ה=5	Nun	נ=50	Koph	ך=500
Vau	ו=6	Samech	ס=60	Mem	ם=600 | Finals
Zayin	ז=7	Ayin	ע=70	Nun	ן=700 | Finals
Cheth	ח=8	Pe	פ=80	Pe	ף=800 | Finals
Teth	ט=9	Tsaddi	צ=90	Tsaddi	ץ=900 | Finals

The Greek Alphabet. The Greek letters were 24, and the required number, 27, was made up by using the final "s" or g (called *Stigma*) for 6, and adding two arbitrary symbols called respectively *Koppa* for 90, and *Sampi* for 900.

Alpha	α =1	Iota	ι =10	Rho	ρ =100
Beta	β =2	Kappa	κ =20	Sigma	σ =200
Gamma	γ =3	Lambda	λ =30	Tau	τ =300
Delta	δ =4	Mu	μ =40	Upsilon	υ =400
Epsilon	ε =5	Nu	ν =50	Phi	φ =500
Stigma	ς =6	Xi	ξ =60	Chi	χ =600
Zeta	ζ =7	Omicron	o =70	Psi	ψ =700
Eta	η =8	Pi	π =80	Omega	ω =800
Theta	*θ* =9	*Koppa*	Ϙ =90	*Sampi*	ϡ =900

Thus if we had the same system in English: A = 1, B = 2, C = 3, D = 4, E = 5 etc. Then the arrangement BAD could be *a word,* meaning 'not good', or a *number, 2 + 1 + 4 = 7.*

In Greek and Hebrew this is exactly what happens. Consider the Greek word for 'and' (*kai,* και). That could be the *word* meaning 'and' or it could be the *number* 20 + 1 + 10 = 31. Thus every Greek and Hebrew word has a numerical value. Every Greek and Hebrew word can also be looked upon as a number - the context decides which it is. This phenomenon is known as Numerics or Numerology. Some find it a most fascinating subject, but we cannot go into great detail here.

Appendix 10 of *The Companion Bible* sets out how certain numbers can be used symbolically in the Bible. For instance:

ONE   DENOTES UNITY AND COMMENCEMENT.
TWO   DENOTES DIFFERENCE AND DIVISION.
THREE   DENOTES COMPLETENESS.
FOUR   DENOTES CREATIVE WORKS.
FIVE   DENOTES DIVINE GRACE.
SIX   DENOTES THE HUMAN NUMBER.
SEVEN   DENOTES SPIRITUAL PERFECTION.
EIGHT   DENOTES RESURRECTION & REGENERATION.
NINE   DENOTES FINALITY AND JUDGEMENT.
TEN   DENOTES ORDINAL PERFECTION.
ELEVEN   DENOTES DISORDER AND DISORGANIZATION.
TWELVE   DENOTES GOVERNMENTAL PERFECTION.
THIRTEEN   DENOTES REBELLION, APOSTAY, DEFECTION,
                   DISINTEGRATION & REVOLUTION.

We will stop there, but perhaps we can now see 'unlucky 13' and 'lucky 7' in a different light. Perhaps, behind the superstitions are biblical truths which have been lost.

Also, we can better appreciate the famous "number of his name" in Revelation 13:17, 18; the number 666. This world-ruler is to be stamped with man's number, the number 6; to have that number three times over shows this person to be the complete human ruler, with all the failings of humanity. As Lord Acton said, "Power corrupts and absolute power corrupts absolutely."

But what will be the name of this ruler? We are not told. All we do know is that the numerical value of that name is 666; but note . . . this phenomenon works for Greek and Hebrew only. In the past people have tried to make it work in German for Hitler and in Italian for Mussolini. No, it must be in Greek or Hebrew and for that very reason some have thought this future world-ruler must be either a Jew or a Greek. But that is not necessarily true. He could be of another nationality but with a Greek or Hebrew name. (For instance, I am British, but Michael is a Hebrew name.)

So we have this dictator with the number 666. Biblical prophecy predicts that the One Who is to defeat him is Jesus (ιησους, iesous).

J	E	S	U		S	
ι	η	σ	ο	υ	ς	
10 +	8 +	200 +	70 +	400 +	200	= 888

Stop for a moment and think. This is quite remarkable! Eight is the number of resurrection and regeneration, and the name Jesus is stamped with three eights – a mere coincidence or divine choice? After all it was the angel, the divine messenger in Matthew 1:21, who said what his name was to be:

> She will give birth to a son, and you are to give him the name Jesus, because he will save his people from their sins.

So the one with the number 888 is to defeat the one with the number 666; but there is more to numeric than that. Consider the following titles of Christ, and check to see if we are correct.

CHRIST	Christos	χριστος	1,480=8x185
LORD	Kurios	χυριος	800=8x100
SAVIOUR	Sōtēr	σωτηρ	1,408=8x8x22
MESSIAH	Messias	μεσσιας	656=8x82
SON	Huios	υίος	680=8x85

So we see that Jesus, his name and many of his titles, are stamped with the number of resurrection and regeneration. Again ... mere coincidence or divine guidance?

We can find more examples of this phenomenon. The number 13 always intrigues people. If we work out the numerics of some of Satan's titles in the Bible we get:

DRAGON	drakōn	δρακων	975=13x75
SERPENT	ophis	οφις	780=13x60
MURDERER	anthrōpoktonos	ανθρωποκτονος	1,820=13x140
TEMPTER	peirazōn	πειραζων	1,053=13x81

The numerical value of the expression 'who is called the Devil and Satan' is 2197, and 2197 = 13 x 13 x 13. Other phrases which contain this number are:

'The mark of the beast' in Revelation 13.17	2483	=13 x 191
'The Mother of the Harlots' in Revelation 17.5	2756	=13 x 212
'The number of the beast' in Revelation 13.18	2067	=13 x 159

All these expressions are obviously associated with evil, and the numerical values emphasize that fact. We could go on and cite many more interesting facts (e.g. Scripture records 13 famines). We could spend much time on each number, (e.g. 7 is a very interesting number, and obviously associated with the Sabbath. How many miracles did Christ perform on Sabbath days? Answer — the Scriptures record 7.)

We suggest that the interested reader obtain a copy of *Number in Scripture* by E. W. Bullinger. This book deals with the subject clearly and objectively and contains a wealth of valuable material — as well as a few arithmetical mistakes! The author does not allow himself to indulge in fantasies, as do some writers on this subject.

A most interesting study of the number 37 and of the interrelationship between 13 and 37 can be found in C. A. Ozanne's *The First 7,000 Years*. In Appendix 1 of that book, it is claimed there will be found:

The most conclusive proof in our possession of the plenary inspiration of the Bible, an inspiration not merely verbal, but literal.

Charles Ozanne also refers to Ivan Panin's pamphlet *The Inspiration of Scriptures Scientifically Demonstrated.* This deals primarily with the first eleven verses of Matthew's gospel. These verses, according to Panin, display the following features:

1. Their *vocabulary* in Greek has 49 words	7 x 7
2. Of these words 28 begin with vowels	4 x 7
3. 21 begin with consonants	3 x 7
4. The 49 words contain 266 letters	38 x 7
5. and 266-7x2x19 and 7+2+19=28	4 x 7
6. Of the 266 letters, 140 are vowels	20 x 7
7. and 126 are consonants	18 x 7
8. Of the 49 words, 35 occur more than once	5 x 7
9. and 14 occur only once	2 x 7
10. Of the 49 words, 7 occur in more than one form	1 x 7
11. and 42 occur in only one form	6 x 7
12. Of the 49 words, 42 are nouns	6 x 7
13. and 7 are not nouns	1 x 7
14. Of the 42 nouns, 35 are names of people	5 x 7
15. and 7 are ordinary nouns	1 x 7
16. Of the 35 names, 28 are male ancestors of Christ	4 x 7
17. and 7 are not ...and so on...	1 x 7

Now this seems incredible, but if you look up a Greek NT text and check it through, you may not find it easy. One mathematician wrote saying that in his Greek text he had found not 49 words but 172, and there were many more than 266 letters. Thus he was left wondering how Panin[8] got the above results.

Close investigation reveals that Panin is *not* talking about the total number of words used. He is talking about the number of *different* words that occur in Matthew 1:1-11, i.e. the *vocabulary* used. Thus the word 'begat' is counted once even though it occurs some 27 times. Abraham is counted once but occurs twice. David is counted once but occurs three times; etc. It is this vocabulary of 49 words, and the 266 letters which make up these words, that Panin considers.

A close examination of most modern NT Greek texts shows that the above is correct. Certainly Panin's analysis of the first chapter of Matthew, and Ozanne's of the first chapter of Genesis, are powerful arguments for the inspiration of Scripture, but we should just mention one point.

In feature 5 above, Panin pointed out that, $266 = 7 \times 2 \times 19$ and that $7 + 2 + 19 = 28$ and that $28 = 4 \times 7$.

We are left wondering whether this has any relevance. That surely is a mere coincidence and should not be included in *objective* evidence. If it is to be included, then so too should be the fact that, in feature, 6,

$140 = 7 \times 2 \times 2 \times 5$ and that $7 + 2 + 2 + 5 = 16$ which is *not* a multiple of 7.

Similarly from feature 7,

$126 = 7 \times 2 \times 3 \times 3$ and $7 + 2 + 3 + 3 = 15$ which is *not* a multiple of 7.

---

[8] Note that Panin used his own 1934 Greek text, *The Numeric Greek New Testament*, which was an adjustment of the 1881 Westcott and Hort text. These edited texts have 137,923 and 137,692 Greek words, respectively.

However the removal of feature 5 does not weaken Panin's case; it strengthens it.

One incorrect piece of arithmetic does not disprove and invalidate the whole of a mathematical problem; neither does one piece of incorrect numeric indicate that the whole of biblical numeric is unreliable. It isn't. It is a difficult subject, but one which demonstrates clearly that behind the different writings of the Bible is a powerful, all-knowing force.

Point 5 – The testimony of structure

Traditional English poetry has metre, rhythm and rhyme, although some modern forms lack all three. Ancient Hebrew poetry, although lacking rhyme, has rhythm and metre; and similar or contrasting thoughts or words are often repeated. This can easily be seen in a few verses from the book of Job, the bulk of which is written in poetical form. Note Job 3:3-9, and compare verse 10. These first seven verses compare and contrast ideas of day and night, light and darkness. In them Job laments, and verse 10 breaks with those ideas and gives the reason for the lament.

May the day of my birth perish,
    and the night it was said,
        'A boy is born!'
That day – may it turn to darkness,
    may God above not care about it,
        may no light shine upon it.
May darkness and deep shadow claim it once more;
    may a cloud settle over it;
        may blackness overwhelm its light.
That night – may thick darkness seize it,
    may it not be included among the days of the year
    nor be entered in any of the months.
May that night be barren;
    may no shout of joy be heard in it.
May those who curse days curse that day,
    those who are ready to rouse Leviathan.
May its morning stars become dark,
    may it wait for daylight in vain

> and not see the first rays of dawn,
> *for it did not shut the doors of the womb on me*
>   *to hide trouble from my eyes.*

Here we can see a pattern or structure in the writing, and this should not come as a surprise in what is a poetical section. But patterns or structures are displayed throughout the whole of the Bible. Every book, every section, displays some feature or other. For example, consider the prophecy of Zacharias contained in Luke 1:68-79 (quoted here from the *KJV*):

68	Blessed be the Lord God of Israel; for he hath <u>visited</u> and redeemed his people,
69	And hath raised up an horn of <u>salvation</u> for us in the house of His servant David;
70	As he spake by the mouth of his holy <u>prophets,</u> which have been since the world began:
71	That we should be saved from our <u>enemies,</u> and from the hand of all that hate us;
72,73	To perform the mercy *promised* to our fathers, and to remember his holy <u>covenant</u>, the oath which he sware to our father Abraham,
74,75	That he would grant unto us, that we being delivered out of the hand of our <u>enemies</u> might serve him without fear, in holiness and righteousness before him, all the days of our life.
76	And thou child, shalt be called the <u>prophet</u> of the highest, for thou shalt go before the face of the Lord to prepare his ways.
77	To give knowledge of <u>salvation</u> unto his people by the remission of their sins.
78,79	Through the tender mercy of our God; whereby the dayspring from on high hath <u>visited</u> us, to give light to them that sit in darkness and *in* the shadow of death, to guide our feet into the way of peace.

Notice, in Luke 1: the word *visited* in verses 68 and 78; the word *salvation* in verses 69 and 77; the word *prophet* in verses 70 and 76; the word *enemies* in verses 71 and 74 and the central word *covenant* in verse 72. We can display the structure more clearly as follows:

68	God has visited.
69	Horn of salvation.
70	His holy prophets.
71	Saved from enemies.
72,73	Remember his covenant.
74, 75	Deliverance from enemies.
76	The prophet.
77	Knowledge of salvation.
78,79	Dayspring has visited.

How was Zacharias' speech so well balanced? Displaying the speech in its structure form shows us the main points and highlights the central feature: 'Remember his holy covenants'. Thus structure helps us in understanding and studying Scripture. But could a human being plan a speech in such a format? The answer is obviously 'Yes!': and it wouldn't be too difficult in a short speech – but in a longer one? That would be putting it above human capabilities. Also, how is it that *all* the biblical writers and speakers display this feature? Consider, as another example, the Epistle of Jude. Read this Epistle, which comes just before the book of Revelation. It has 25 verses and its structure is as follows:

1,2	Introduction.
3	**Beloved,** contend for the *faith*.
4	**Ungodly** of 'old'.
5	**Remembrance** of the Lord's acts.
5-16	5-8 *3 examples*. Israel, Angels, Sodom.
	9-10 Michael[9].
	11-13 *3 examples*. Cain,Balaam,Korah.
	14-16 The Lord's coming[10].
17	**Remembrance** of the Lord's words.
18,19	**Ungodly** of last times'.
20-23	**Beloved,** build on *faith*.
24,25	Doxology.

It must have taken Jude quite some time to write such a fluent letter, yet displaying such symmetry – unless of course a higher power was carrying him along!

Space does not permit us to display the full structure of, say, a Gospel; but in Appendix 5 we reproduce from Appendix 176 of *The Companion Bible,* 'The Eight Signs of John's Gospel [John 2:1-11...21:1-14]'. Look at that structure of these signs and ask is it at all possible for a man like John, in his account of the ministry of the Lord Jesus Christ, to exhibit such perfect symmetry? Probably not, and we are inclined to ask if John was one of the holy men of God who, as Peter wrote, was carried along by the Holy Spirit. (Appendix 6 contains the structure of Ephesians, {1:3-3:13; 3:14-21; 4:1-6:24}.)

In concluding this section we quote from the Preface to *The Companion Bible* where it states "The structures ... require a special note" which states:

---

[9] Not recorded in the Bible, but mentioned in the Apocryphal *Assumptions of Moses*

[10] Not directly recorded in the Bible, but mentioned in the Apocryphal *Book of Enoch*.

They give, not a mere *Analysis* evolved from the text by human ingenuity, but *a Symmetrical exhibition* of the Word itself, which may be discerned by the humblest reader of the Sacred Text, and seen to be one of the most important evidences of the Divine Inspiration of its words.

Some would claim that this feature is due solely to the style of writing dominant at the time; but when we realize that the writers of the Bible cover a period of over 1,500 years, this seems extremely unlikely.

Point 6 – The Testimony of the Lord Jesus Christ

Those of us who claim to be Christians, i.e. followers of Christ, might be interested to know how he treated the Scriptures. Naturally his followers, his servants, his disciples should display a similar attitude; for he said:

A student is not above his teacher,
>   nor is a servant above his master.
It is enough for the student to be like his teacher, and
>   the servant like his master.
(Matthew 10:24-25)

Note: The student is *not* above his teacher and the servant is *not* above his master. It is enough for the student to be *like his teacher,* and the servant *like his master.* These are words to be followed by all who claim to be Christians. So....

What was *The* Teacher's attitude to the Scriptures? What was *The* Master's view of them? Ours should be the same.

One of the first comments the Lord Jesus made upon the Scriptures is found in Matthew 5:17-18:

Do not think I have come to abolish the Law and the Prophets; I have not come to abolish them but to fulfil them. I tell you the truth, until heaven and earth disappear, not the smallest letter, not the least stroke of a pen, will by any means disappear from the Law until everything is accomplished.

The smallest Hebrew letter is the *yod*, equivalent to the Greek *iota* or the English *i* or *y*. The stroke of the pen referred to is the *tittle*, a small ornament added to certain Hebrew letters, but carefully tabulated in the Massorah. Here the Lord assures them that neither the smallest letter nor the tiniest ornament shall fail to be fulfilled. The Lord Jesus Christ could not have given stronger support to the Law and the Prophets. Another statement of Christ is found in John 5:46-47.

> If you believed Moses, you would believe me, for he wrote about me. But since you do not believe what he wrote, how are you going to believe what I say?

What a supreme testimony to the writings of Moses! Here the Lord Jesus was speaking to certain Jews of his day who didn't believe what Moses wrote, and especially didn't believe what Moses wrote about Christ. Here the Lord Jesus does not beat about the bush.

> Since you do not believe what he wrote, how are you going to believe what I say? (John 5:47)

These words are still a challenge to every Christian today. If we don't believe what Moses wrote, how can we believe what Christ said? How can we trust in and rely on what the Lord Jesus said unless we believe Moses? We cannot, for at every opportunity he supported the writings of Moses.

> ...if they do not listen to Moses and the Prophets, they will not be convinced even if someone rises from the dead. (Luke 16:31)

These are the words that Christ puts into the account of the Rich Man and Lazarus. Here he presents the testimony of the writings of Moses and the prophets as of greater persuasive power than the mighty miracle of raising the dead.

This was also Peter's attitude. He had been present at Christ's Transfiguration (Luke 9:28-36) and wrote about it in his second epistle, (2 Peter 1:16-18). This must have been a tremendous experience for Peter yet he goes on to say:

We have also a more sure word of prophecy . . . (2 Peter 1:19; *KJV*)

And Peter continues to talk about the prophets of the Old Testament. To him their writings were more sure than what he had seen. Thus we who call ourselves Christians can learn a valuable lesson from Peter, who was being a true disciple, student and servant, emulating exactly his Lord's attitude towards the Scriptures. Throughout the whole of his ministry Christ gave authority to the Scripture.

The Scripture cannot be broken. (John 10:35)

Again, Matthew 26 contains Christ's trial before the high priest who asked,

I charge you under oath by the living God: Tell us if you are the Christ, the Son of God. (Matthew 26:63)

How does the Lord Jesus reply? What does he say? He quotes from the book of the prophet Daniel 7:13.

"Yes, it is as you say," Jesus replied. "But I say to all of you: In the future you will see the Son of Man sitting on the right hand of the Mighty One and coming on the clouds of heaven." (Matthew 26:64)

At that solemn moment, Christ quoted Daniel. What a testimony to that book! It obviously met with his full approval.

In an earlier chapter of Matthew, the Lord Jesus Christ said of that generation: "In them is fulfilled the prophecy of Isaiah" (Matthew 13:14). And he goes on to quote Isaiah 6:9-10.

In Mark 7:6, the Lord Jesus said: "Isaiah was right when he prophesied about you hypocrites." And he goes on to quote Isaiah 29:13. In Luke 4:17-21 Christ quotes from Isaiah 61:1-2 and finishes by saying: "Today is this scripture fulfilled in *your* hearing."

We see, here, Christ's endorsement of Isaiah, and we could give many more examples of his complete support for the Old Testament Scriptures; but enough have been given to show that he backed them totally. We will, however, give three further examples of a slightly different nature.

When John the Baptist was in prison, he sent his disciples to ask Christ, "Are you the one who was to come, or should we expect someone else?" (Matthew 11:3). Christ did not answer the question directly. His answer is again an appeal to Scripture, to the book of Isaiah. The miracles, that Christ told John's disciples to tell John about, were the very signs that Isaiah prophesied that the Messiah would do.

> Be strong, do not fear; your God will come,
> he will come with vengeance; with divine retribution
> he will come to save you.
> Then will the eyes of the blind be opened
> and the ears of the deaf unstopped.
> Then will the lame leap like a deer,
> and the mute tongue shout for joy.
> (Isaiah 35:4-6; compare Matthew 11:4-6; Isaiah 29:18; 61:1)

Again, the temptations in the wilderness provide an excellent example of the authority of the Scriptures. Here Christ overcomes the adversary; not by the power of his Godhead, but by the power of God's Word. Each temptation is met with, "It is written," (Matthew 4:4, 7, 10). The first temptation is dispelled with a quotation from Deuteronomy 8:3; the second by a quote from Deuteronomy 6:16; and the third with one from Deuteronomy 6:13. Can anything be a greater testimony to the power and authority of Scripture?

We may think that when he was on earth, as a man, he was limited to the knowledge of his day. But was he? Note John 2:24-25:

But Jesus would not entrust himself to them, for he knew all men. He did not need man's testimony about man, for he knew what was in a man.

Are we to assume that in those days it was common for people to know 'what was in a man'? We think not. Such a view is not tenable. This shows that Christ had superior knowledge when on earth; but we should also note that, after his resurrection, Christ made the following claim:

All authority in heaven and on earth has been given to me. (Matthew 28:18)

How did this raised, glorified and authoritative Christ treat the Scriptures? Had he changed his mind? Had he revised his beliefs?

He said unto them, "How foolish you are, and how slow of heart to believe all that the prophets have spoken. Did not Christ have to suffer these things and then enter his glory?" And beginning with Moses and all the Prophets, he explained to them what was said in *all the Scriptures* concerning himself. (Luke 24:25-27)

This was addressed to the two on the Emmaus road. To the eleven, he said:

"This is what I told you while I was still with you: Everything must be fulfilled that is written about me in the Law of Moses, the Prophets and the Psalms." Then he opened their minds so they could understand the Scriptures. (Luke 24:44-45)

These are not the words of one who doubted the authority of Scripture. These are the words of one who fully and completely endorsed the authority, reliability and accuracy of the Word of God. Remember, "the student is not above the teacher, and the servant is not above the master." Surely everyone who calls himself a Christian – a follower of Christ – must have the same attitude towards the Scriptures as that exhibited by his Lord and Master.

We see that the Apostles did just that; but some theologians, wishing to uphold their ideas, have questioned the integrity of the Apostles' writings and behaviour. They will justify this by such statements because they consider themselves pygmies standing on the shoulders of giants, and that enables them to see a little further and a little clearer. However 21st century theologians, looking back nearly 2000 years, are not necessarily going to see and understand what happened as clearly as the Apostles who lived at the time! (For more on this see Appendix 1).

Point 7 – The testimony of the writers

What do the writers of the Bible say about the writings? This may appear to be a strange question, but it is one that should be considered. Did they think that the writings were inspired? Did they think God spoke through them?

(1) PAUL'S TESTIMONY

In 2 Timothy 4:6-7, Paul wrote:

> For I am already being poured out like a drink offering, and the time has come for my departure. I have fought the good fight, I have finished the race, I have kept the faith.

Paul was soon to be put to death, probably by the sword. He knew the time was approaching, so he wrote to Timothy. What was on his mind? What was important to him?

> ... from infancy you have known the holy Scriptures, which are able to make you wise for salvation through faith in Christ Jesus. All Scripture is God-breathed and is useful for teaching, rebuking, correcting, and training in righteousness, so that the man of God may be thoroughly equipped for every good work. (2 Timothy 3:15-17)

To Paul, what was written was God-breathed. There was no interval to allow the writer to cloud the divine message with his own ideas, yet the writer's personal style was preserved.

In the past God spoke to our forefathers through the prophets at many times and in *various ways*. (Hebrews 1:1)

Thus the various ways allowed for the different styles of the prophets and writers. The style of presentation was diverse but the originator of the message was God.

(2) PETER'S TESTIMONY

Similarly, Peter knew that he was to be put to death (2 Peter 1:13-14) and with this in mind what did he write about? Verses 16-18 of that same chapter deal with the Transfiguration, and we mentioned earlier how Peter, in verse 19, stated, "We have also a more sure word of prophecy,..."(*KJV*). He goes on to state:

Above all, you must understand that no prophecy of Scripture came about by the prophet's own interpretation. For prophecy never had its origin in the will of man, but men spoke from God, as they were carried along by the Holy Spirit. (2 Peter 1:20-21)

The word translated *carried along* in 2 Peter 1:21 occurs twice in Acts 27, verses 15 and 17. There, in a vivid description of a ship being wrecked, the same word is translated *driven along*.

The ship was caught by the storm and could not head into the wind; so we gave way to it and were *driven along* ... Fearing that they would run aground on the sand-bars of Syrtis, they lowered the sea anchor and let the ship be *driven along*. (Acts 27:15, 17)

In that storm the ship was helpless. The human element could not interfere; it *could do nothing* to alter the course of the ship. Similarly the human writer through whom God spoke was *driven along* by the Holy Spirit. The human element could not interfere with or affect or change the truth of that message. These were Peter's speeches recorded in the book of Acts:

Brothers, the Scriptures had to be fulfilled which the Holy Spirit spake long ago through the mouth of David concerning Judas. (Acts 1:16, referring to Psalm 69.)

But this is how God fulfilled what he had foretold through all the prophets, saying that his Christ would suffer. (Act 3:18, referring to *all* the prophets.)

He must remain in heaven until the time comes for *God* to restore everything, as he *promised* long ago *through his holy prophets.*" (Acts 3:21, again referring to 'all' his prophets, {as the *KJV* makes clear}.)

(3) MATTHEW'S TESTIMONY

MATTHEW 1:22: All this took place to fulfil *what the Lord had said through the prophet.* (Matthew 1:23 quotes Isaiah 7:14.)
MATTHEW 2:15: And so was fulfilled *what the Lord has said through* the prophet. (And the same verse quotes Hosea 11:1)
MATTHEW 2:23: So was fulfilled what was said *through the prophets.* (And the rest of the verse quotes the prophets, plural; though Isaiah 11:1 and 60:21 also refer.)
MATTHEW 21:4: This took place to fulfil what was spoken *through the prophet.* (And the rest of the verse quotes Zechariah 9:9.)

We could give many more examples (e.g. Matthew 2:5-6 and its support for Micah 5:2, Matthew 27:9 and its support for what was said by Jeremiah); but there is sufficient here to show that Matthew considered that the prophets were but the mouthpiece of God. No matter who the individual speaker was or how he wrote it, the message came from God.

(4) MOSES' TESTIMONY

EXODUS 4:12: "Now therefore go, and I will be with thy "Now therefore go, and I will be with thy <u>mouth</u>, and teach thee what thou shalt say." (*KJV*)
NUMBERS 12:8: "With him will I speak <u>mouth to mouth,</u>..." (*KJV*)
NUMBERS 23:5: The Lord put a word in Balaam's <u>mouth,</u> ... *(KJV)*

God putting words in the mouth is also mentioned by the prophets, e.g. Isaiah 51:16; Jeremiah 1:9 and 2 Chronicles 36:22.

We could go on (for example, the expression 'thus saith Lord' occurs over four hundred times in the Old Testament), but we have given enough here to show that the writers themselves considered their writings, and those of the other apostles and prophets, to be the words of God. Do we accept their testimony?

Point 8 – Ring of truth

Some people are swayed by mighty arguments, but others are convinced by one or two small but telling truths. We have not dealt with the actual teachings of the Bible. We have not considered the biblical view of man or its philosophy of life, although many are convinced about the inspiration of Scriptures because of what it says about life and the nature of man. What it says about such things as these has a 'ring of truth' and from that many are prepared to generalize outward and accept that the Bible is true in everything it deals with. So, what does the Bible say about man?

All have sinned and fall short of the glory of God. (Romans 3:23)

We hear little, nowadays, about the sinful nature of man, for we like to blame the faults of an individual upon the failings of society. Unsociable behaviour, we are tempted to say, is the fault of the society and not of the individual. *But society is merely a collection of individuals.* Thus all this view does is shift the responsibility, the blame and the crime or failure, from one set of shoulders to another. The plain truth is that we live in a world which contains sinful people, and this writer is one of them. But let's be clear over the meaning of this world 'sin'. As soon as sin is mentioned, people start to think of swearing, fighting, fornication, drunkenness, violence and the like. Yet the true meaning of the word is given in Romans 3:23:

All have sinned and fall short of the glory of God.

If we fall short of the glory of God, we sin. That's it. None of us is perfect as God is perfect. Thus the society we form cannot be perfect. We come short, so our society comes short. This is the truth and we all know it, deep down. We may not like it, but it is true. Man is imperfect and the society we form is imperfect, yet the remedy for putting that society right is so easy. Bertrand Russell wrote:

> If we could all learn to *love our neighbor* the world would quickly become a paradise for us all.

It may seem strange that even an atheistic philosopher like Bertrand Russell can see the truth of the biblical command "Thou shalt love thy neighbour as thyself" in Leviticus 19:18. Many know that it makes sense and it has that 'ring of truth'. Thus to improve society is so easy – to say. However, it is so difficult – to do! Why? Why can't people love their neighbours as themselves? Firstly because, as the Lord Jesus Christ said in Matthew 22:39, "that is the second great commandment." The first great commandment, which needs to be carried out beforehand, is:

> Love the Lord your God with all your heart and with all your soul and with all your mind. (Matthew 22:37; from Deuteronomy 6:5, 10:12, 30:6)

Therefore we need first to love God so that we can have the will, the power and the strength to love our neighbours, and here we mean biblical love, that self-sacrificing love that Christ had, and care about people. The Bible goes on to say that ....

> ... the wages of sin is death. (Romans 6:23)

The cost of sin, the price of sin and the result of sin is death. No one needs proof that we all sin; and no one needs proof that we all die. However, this verse in Romans links these two together and goes on to state:

> ... but the gift of God is eternal life in Christ Jesus our Lord.

This, too, is an obvious truth, for unless God did something, the grave would be the final resting-place for us all – but it isn't.

So in all these matters, and in many others relating to man, the Bible has the ring of truth. It may not be palatable to a post-modernist and permissive society, it may not be accepted by a materialistic and self-seeking world, but everyone, deep down, knows that the Bible, on man's nature and man's fate, is speaking the truth.

AGNOSTIC – One who holds that nothing is known, or likely to be known, of the existence of God or of anything beyond material phenomena.

One who believes that the existence of God and of life hereafter can neither be proved nor disproved, and who accepts only material phenomena.

One agnostic argument is that one cannot tell whether there was a God because it is impossible for finite man to search, communicate with and contact the infinite God. This is indeed a logical and powerful argument and can be traced to Zophar the Naamathite, one of Job's friends. He said (Job 11:7):

Can you fathom the mysteries of God?
Can you prove the limits of the Almighty? (*NIV*)

Canst thou by searching find out God?
Canst thou find out the Almighty unto perfection? (*KJV*)

These are all rhetorical questions which demand the answer 'NO!' No. One cannot find out the limits of the Almighty because one cannot, by searching, even find him.

He has also set eternity in the hearts of men; yet they cannot fathom what God has done from the beginning to the end. (Ecclesiastes 3:11)

It looks here as if there is more evidence for the agnostic case! And even more seems to come from the New Testament.

> No eye has seen, no ear has heard, no mind has conceived what God has prepared for those who love him.
> (1 Corinthians 2:9)

So speaks Zophar in the book of Job, Solomon in Ecclesiastes and Paul in 1 Corinthians – are they agreeing with the agnostic argument? It is certainly true that finite man cannot search out and contact the infinite God but...the infinite God can 'ever so easily' reach out and contact finite man. If he couldn't, he wouldn't be infinite, he wouldn't be God. But let's quote Paul's next verse in 1 Corinthians 2:9-10.

> No eye has seen,
> >no ear has heard,
> no mind has conceived
> >what God has prepared for those who love him.
> **But God has revealed it to us by his Spirit.**

This is just the point! God is omnipotent (all-powerful) and if he isn't, then he isn't God. For the all-powerful God to inspire men to write his words and to ensure that these writings are collected and collated into one book is, for him, a trivial exercise. If we have difficulty with this, then the phrase, coined elsewhere in a title of a book, *Your God is Too Small*, by J. B. Phillips, may sum up our real problem. Belief in the inspiration of the Scriptures is tied up with our view of God. It is only an atheist who can reject the inspiration of the Bible on the grounds that such a thing is impossible. The believer in God must subscribe, not merely to the possibility, or even the probability, but to the certainty of that truth; for would a God of love leave generations without clear guidance? We think not.

Point 10 – Contradictions?

We may think that the Bible cannot be inspired because we have heard that it contains contradictions. But does it? Obviously God's instructions to one group of people at one time may be different from his will for the same group of people at another time, or for a totally different group of people. However, these are not contradictions.

When Miles Coverdale produced the first printed Bible in English in 1535, he was aware that people would have difficulty in establishing the correct interpretation of passages. He wrote the following:

> It shall greatly helpe ye to understande Scripture,
> if thou mark,
>> not only what is spoken, or wrytten,
> but of whom,
>> and to whom,
> with what words,
>> at what time [when?],
> Where,
>> to what intent [why?],
> with what circumstance,
>> considering what goeth before,
> and what followeth.[11]

Thus all Scripture must not only be taken in its context, but we must also know to whom it was addressed and when it was given; it helps us to know the reason (to what intent) and the circumstances.

For example, early on in his ministry, when the Lord Jesus Christ sent out the Twelve, his instructions were:

> Take nothing for the journey – no staff, no bag, no bread, no money, no extra shirt. (Luke 9:3)

This was repeated when, a little while later, he went out the seventy two.

> Do not take a purse or bag or sandals. (Luke 10:4)

---

[11] I have given a full explanation of this quote, together with its implications, in the book *Approaching the Bible*, published by the Open Bible Trust.

However, just before his crucifixion, he knew the situation was going to change. He called his disciples together and said to them:

> "When I sent you without purse, bag or sandals, did you lack anything?" "Nothing," they answered. He said to them, "But now if you have a purse, take it, and also a bag; and if you don't have a sword, sell your cloak and buy one." (Luke 22:35-36)

To try to live in accordance with Luke 9:3 and 10:4, as some missionaries and Christian workers do, is to ignore what Christ said later.

From the day they left Egypt, the people of Israel sacrificed the Passover lamb once every year. However, when Christ, the Passover Lamb, had been slain...we see no mention of Christian Jews keeping this feast in the Bible from that time onward, although throughout the Acts of the Apostles the Jewish Christians, like Paul, kept certain other feasts (see Acts 18:21 *KJV*, probably Tabernacles.) And the Christian Jews continued the practice of circumcision (see Acts 16:1-5, and this is discussed in Appendix 1).

But what about the Gentile Christians in the Acts of the Apostles? Did they have to keep such feasts, and other parts of the Mosaic Law such as circumcision? No. This was an issue of the Jerusalem Council, recorded in Acts 15, and their decision was that:

> It seemed good to the Holy Spirit and to us not to burden you with anything beyond the following requirements: You are to abstain from food sacrificed to idols, from blood, from the meat of strangled animals and from sexual immorality. You will do well to avoid these things. (Acts 15:28-29)

Thus, depending on the time and upon the people concerned, God may give different instructions, but these are not contradictory. It is an all wise God, the Father who loves his children, who sees the different needs and requirements of his different children at different times. The principle of Miles Coverdale, stated above, removes those apparent contradictions.

In Conclusion

We have presented in this chapter several sets of evidence to substantiate the divine origin of the Bible. We have attempted to be objective in our choice of evidence and in the way it has been presented. We have considered:

Point 1 –Facts recorded before they were known
Point 2 –The Testimony of Prophecy
Point 3 –The Testimony of Probability
Point 4 –The Testimony of Numerics
Point 5 –The Testimony of Structure
Point 6 –The Testimony of the Lord Jesus
Point 7 –The Testimony of the Writers
Point 8 –Ring of Truth
Point 9 –The Agnostic Argument
Point 10-Contradictions

None of the above subjects has been dealt with exhaustively, for each one would merit a book, but we hope we have given sufficient to show that each is not a flight of fancy. Interested readers can follow up any line of study and research it for themselves and, if they do so, they can be assured of some exciting and stimulating discoveries.

Any one of the above points, by itself, may be sufficient to convince some people that the Bible is the inspired Word of God. Any two should convince many more people but as one friend wrote:

> I wonder what are the chances of
> Prophetic fulfilment,
> Numerics and
> Structures
> *all* occurring together in one piece of literature?

The point is reinforced further when we note that the Bible was written by over forty people coming from a variety of backgrounds and over a period of time covering over 1,500 years.

Final Questions

Does anyone still think the Bible is not worth believing? Does anyone still think that the Bible is merely a collection of the writings of men, on a par with other literature? Does anyone still think the Bible is not inspired? Does anyone still think that the Bible is not God's Word?

Postscript: The Bible is *the* Authority

So what is our view of the Bible? Do we see it as a unique book and a reliable book? Do we believe it to be an inspired book? Whatever our view, if we are Christians then the Bible is *the* authority.

We may believe that although the original autographs (the original documents when they were first written down) *were* inspired and inerrant, we know man allowed errors to creep in, due to the copying process. None the less, the Bible is still *the* authority.

Some get quite uncomfortable when 21st century theologians question the authority and integrity of the 1st century Apostles and what they wrote. These theologians come out with statements that they are but pygmies standing on the shoulders of the apostolic giants, and claim that in that position they can see further and clearer. Although such a statement may be true in subjects like Mathematics or Physics or Astronomy, it may well be unsound and unsafe to apply it to such issues as to what happened and what was taught in the distant past.

People today, looking back 2,000 years, may have a better understanding than those who lived 1,000 years ago. However, they are not going to see more clearly than those who walked and talked with Jesus (before and after his resurrection). They are not going to have a better understanding than those who came on the scene ten to twenty years afterwards, like Paul and Titus. (For more on this see Appendix 1.)

We may not fully understand all that those Apostles wrote and some of it may be ambiguous to us, but their documents, their doctrines, their descriptions of what happened, are the best we have, far better than some of the 'new' thinking of today and the recent past..

So whatever our view of the Bible as a book, whether we believe it inspired or not, we need to appreciate that it is the most authoritative document that we have *in the world*, and we need to accept is as such.

Appendix 1: The Integrity of the Apostles and their Writings

There are some Christians who, in an attempt to justify their theology or their 'new' understanding of the Bible, cast doubt on the integrity of the Apostles. The Bible does not hide the failures of its main characters. Paul and Barnabas argued so vociferously over John Mark that they parted company, but later Paul was willing to work with Mark (Acts 15:36-40; Colossians 4:10; 2 Timothy 4:11).

Many know of Peter's denials, but he also made a serious error in Antioch when, under pressure from the Judaisers, he refused to eat with Gentile Christians (Galatians 2:11-14). However a little while later, at the Jerusalem Council (Acts 15:6-11), he stood side-by-side with Paul and argued strongly against those who would have Gentile Christians be circumcised and keep the Law of Moses.

Thus we find these wonderful men of God, when under pressure, may say or do the wrong thing – just like all of us. However, in the cold light of day, after reflection, we find them doing and saying the right thing.

But some use these isolated indiscretions to cast doubt on the integrity of their teaching, decisions and actions. We give three examples of where, to justify their understanding of what went on just after our Lord's time on earth, some criticise the actions and decisions of the Apostles, and disagree with their teaching.

The Great Commission

Go and make disciples of all nations, baptizing them in the name of the Father and of the Son and of the Holy Spirit, and teaching them to obey everything I have commanded you. (Matthew 28:19-20)

This, say some, the Apostles never did. They simply stayed in Jerusalem and were forced into Samaria by the persecution of the Jerusalem Church by Saul of Tarsus. However, if we read the account correctly, we see that even then the Apostles did not leave Jerusalem; they stayed there (see Acts 8:1). This being the case, why did the Apostles stubbornly stay in Jerusalem?

Years later, Paul and Barnabas met them in Jerusalem, and an agreement was made between these two and Peter, James and John. In Galatians 2:9 we read:

They (James, Peter and John) agreed that we (Paul and Barnabas) should go to the Gentiles, and they to the Jews.

However, we need to be careful how we understand this agreement. The Greek for 'Gentiles' is *ethnos* which can have the meaning of 'nations'; and this, perhaps, is how we should understand the agreement. Paul and Barnabas were to go to the 'nations' and preach the gospel to the peoples there, while the Apostles were to stay in Jerusalem and Judea and preach the gospel there.

Certainly, if we follow through Paul's missionary journey that is what he did. He did not simply minister to Gentile *people*. He went to Gentile *nations* and ministered to both the Jews and the Gentiles in those countries, nearly always going to the Jewish synagogue first.

But why were the Apostles so insistent upon staying in Jerusalem, and what about the Great Commission? The problem may be with the translation of Matthew 28:19.

In the *NIV* we read "go and make disciples *of* all nations" and some, understandably, interpret this to mean people of all different nationalities. However, *Young's Literal Translation, The Englishman's Greek New Testament,* and various other translations have, simply, "disciple all nations".

I would suggest this means "go and make disciples *from* (or *out of*) all nations", rather than "go and make disciples *of* all nations". The difference may appear small; but it is, in fact, quite considerable. The former "*from* (or *out of*) all nations", would imply that the commission given was for the eleven to witness to the Jewish dispersion, who were scattered amongst the nations. Thus to "disciple all nations" meant making disciples from the Jews of those nations. This, I suggest, is nearer the truth of *the Great Commission* because this was the thrust of the eleven's work, as is recorded in the Acts of the Apostles. (Michael Penny, *40 Problem Passages,* page 102)

They did, in fact, make thousands and thousands of Jewish disciples 'out of' all nations'.

Consider the Pentecost of Acts 2. In verses 5-11 we read:

Now there were staying in Jerusalem God-fearing Jews from every nation under heaven. ...Parthians, Medes and Elamites; residents of Mesopotamia, Judea and Cappadocia, Pontus and Asia, Phrygia and Pamphylia, Egypt and the parts of Libya near Cyrene; visitors from Rome (both Jews and converts to Judaism); Cretans and Arabs.

After Peter preached, we read that there were 'three thousand' who believed, and the number of men who believed soon rose to 'five thousand' (Acts 2:41; 4:4). What did these Jewish believers do? Clearly they returned to their own countries and cities. There, in their local synagogues, they told people about Jesus of Nazareth, and so churches began. The church at Rome began before Paul had visited it. We know this because Aquila and Priscilla, Jewish Christians, had been expelled from Rome by Claudius and met Paul in Corinth on his second missionary journey (Acts 18:1-2).

But who started the church at Rome? Probably some of the Jews from Rome who had been converted at the Pentecost of Acts 2. Similarly the church in Egypt. Some Coptic Christians today state that the church in Egypt was probably started by Mark visiting Egypt in AD 68. However, there were Jews from Egypt, over 35 years earlier, who had heard Peter preach on that day of Pentecost.

But the Pentecost of Acts 2 was not the only feast day in Jerusalem. There were a number each year, where Jews from the known world travelled to worship at the temple. There they would meet Peter and James and John and the Apostles; and there they would hear the message, and a number would believe. By the time we get to Acts 21 James and the elders could tell Paul:

> You see, brother, how many thousands of Jews have believed. (Acts 21:20)

But the Greek says *murias*, myriads, tens of thousands, a large number; (see margin of the *New American Standard Bible*). And by the time Paul wrote to the Colossians we read:

> All over this world this gospel is bearing fruit and growing. (Colossians 1:6)

At the start of Acts, the risen Christ told them, "You will be my witnesses in Jerusalem, and in all Judea and Samaria, and to the ends of the earth," (Acts 1:8). But twice he told them to stay in Jerusalem (Luke 24:49; Acts 1:4). Some see this as an injunction for them to stay for just a little while; but their ministry was confined mainly to that city and the surrounding area, and yet...they were witnesses to the ends of the earth because the world, in the person of the Jewish Dispersion, came to them. And so the Apostles fulfilled the Great Commission, not in the way some modern theologians think they should have, but in the way God wanted them to do so.

James, the Elders and Paul

Our second example also comes from Acts 21. Here James and the Elders are criticised, along with Paul.

On his missionary journeys, and elsewhere, Paul had vigorously defended the position of the Jerusalem Council that the *Gentiles* did not need to be circumcised or keep the Law of Moses. Somehow or other this had been distorted and it had been reported in Jerusalem that Paul had been teaching the *Jews* that they need not be circumcised and keep the Law. To dispel the falsehood of this statement, James and the Elders told Paul to make a Nazirite vow, which involved sacrifices.

> Do what we tell you. There are four men with us who have made a vow. Take these men, join in their purification rites and pay their expenses, so that they can have their heads shaved. Then everyone will know there is no truth in these reports about you, but that you yourself are living in obedience to the law. As for the Gentile believers, we have written to them our decision that they should abstain from food sacrificed to idols, from blood, from the meat of strangled animals and from sexual immorality. (Acts 21:23-25)

The next day Paul took the men and purified himself along with them. Then he went to the temple to give notice of the date when the days of purification would end and the offering would be made for each of them. (Acts 21:23-26)

This raises many issues.

First, says some, that Paul, in his letters stated that people were not 'under the law' of Moses – so he was hypocritical to agree to such a vow. However, what did Paul mean by not being 'under the law'? He certainly did not mean that the Jewish Christians, at that time, need not keep the law. If we look at Paul's own life we see him clearly keeping the Law of Moses on many occasions. Consider, for example, the following:

Paul kept the Sabbath day – see Acts 13:14; 16:13; 17:2; 18:4.

Paul practiced circumcision – see Acts 16:3.
Paul had earlier taken a Nazirite vow – see Acts 18:18.
Paul observed the feasts of Unleavened Bread and Pentecost – see Acts 20:6; 20:16. (And others; Acts 18:21 *KJV*)
Paul respected the position of the high priest – see Acts 23:5.
Paul was concerned to be ceremonially clean – see acts 24:18.

So what did Paul mean about not being 'under the law'. In Galatians 3:10 he wrote about those who "**rely** on observing the law" for obtaining righteousness, being doomed. It would seem that some considered themselves 'under the law', so as to obtain righteousness in God's eyes. It was probably right, at that time, for Jewish Christians to 'observe' the Law; but they were not 'under' the Law for righteousness. They were saved by grace through faith; and, just like Abraham who believed God, their faith was counted for righteousness.

As we have seen, Paul, himself, kept the Law, but why did he and the other Jewish Christians do so? We need to remember that the Jewish Christians needed to witness to those Jews who had not yet accepted Jesus as their Messiah (Christ), Son of God and Savior. If the Jewish Christians no longer kept the Sabbath, if they did not circumcise their baby boys, if they ate the meat of unclean animals or strangled animals, the non-Christian Jews would have had nothing to do with them, and would not listen to them, and would call them 'Gentile dogs'. Thus it was imperative, at that time, for Paul, James, the Elders, the Apostles and all Jewish Christians to observe the Law – not as a means of righteousness, but as a worthy walk to enable them to witness in their own community.

Thus the initial accusation, made by some in the 21st century, is totally unfounded. However, as we progress through the New Testament in time...we find at the end of the Acts an important change.

The Jewish leadership had opposed Christ while he was on earth and had him crucified.

The Jewish leadership opposed Peter and John in their ministry at the start of Acts, imprisoned them and flogged them.

The Jewish leadership had opposed Paul in the synagogues he preached in during his missionary journeys, having him imprisoned, beaten and stoned.

And in about AD 62 the Jewish leadership had James, the Lord's brother, and the Christian leaders in Jerusalem stoned to death. (See Josephus, *Antiquities*, 20, 9, 1).

At the end of the Acts period, about the time James was being stoned in Jerusalem, Paul visited Rome. God's verdict on the Jewish leadership in particular was that because of their hardened hearts they were blind and deaf and could no longer be of service and, for the last time; so Paul quoted Isaiah's prophecy:

> "'Go to this people and say,
> "You will be ever hearing but never understanding;
>   you will be ever seeing but never perceiving."
>
> For this people's heart has become calloused;
>   they hardly hear with their ears,
>   and they have closed their eyes.
> Otherwise they might see with their eyes,
>   hear with their ears,
>   understand with their hearts
> and turn, and I would heal them.'
>
> "Therefore I want you to know that God's salvation has been sent to the Gentiles, and they will listen!"
> (Acts 28:25-28)

That last verse is significant, and heralds a great change. We read that Paul spent the next two years in prison in Rome (Acts 28:30). It was during those two years that he wrote Ephesians and Colossians. It is in those letters that we read:

> For he himself is our peace, who has made the two one and has destroyed the barrier, the dividing wall of hostility, by abolishing in

his flesh the law with its commandments and regulations. His purpose was to create in himself one new man out of the two, thus making peace, and in this one body to reconcile both of them to God through the cross, by which he put to death their hostility. (Ephesians 2:14-16)

...having canceled the written code, with its regulations, that was against us and that stood opposed to us; he took it away, nailing it to the cross. And having disarmed the powers and authorities, he made a public spectacle of them, triumphing over them by the cross.

Therefore do not let anyone judge you by what you eat or drink, or with regard to a religious festival, a New Moon celebration or a Sabbath day. These are a shadow of the things that were to come; the reality, however, is found in Christ. (Colossians 2:14-17)

So it is not until the end of the Acts that God announces, through the ministry of Paul, that the Law was abolished. To read this back into the Acts, and so question the integrity of James, the Elders and Paul, does a great disservice to those men, all of whom gave their lives for Christ.

Who is Jesus?

There are a number of seemingly Christian writers and teachers, who do not believe in the virgin birth, the resurrection; and who deny the deity of Christ. In a desire to harmonise all religions and make them equal paths to God, they have downgraded the Lord Jesus Christ to the status of a prophet, at best, or a mere man, at worst.

They try to uphold a respect for the Apostles by saying that they were giants. However, they go on to say that they, themselves, are pygmies standing on the shoulders of the apostolic giants, and thus they can see a little clearer and further. Even if that were the case, modern day theologians, looking back over nearly 2,000 years, are likely to have far less of a clear view than those who walked and talked with Christ, before and after his resurrection, or of people like Paul, who came on the scene 10 years after Christ rose from the dead and ascended into heaven. What was their view of Jesus? We will quote just a few verses.

Matthew 1:23: "The virgin will be with child and will give birth to a son, and they will call him Immanuel"—which means, 'God with us'."

John 1:1: In the beginning was the Word, and the Word was with God, and the Word was God.

Luke 1:35: "The angel answered, "The Holy Spirit will come upon you, and the power of the Most High will overshadow you. So the holy one to be born will be called the Son of God."

John 5:18: For this reason the Jews tried all the harder to kill him; not only was he breaking the Sabbath, but he was even calling God his own Father, making himself equal with God.

Philippians 2:5-6: Christ Jesus, who, being in very nature God.

Titus 2:13: ... we wait for the blessed hope—the glorious appearing of our great God and Savior, Jesus Christ.

Appendix 2:
Luke's Census and Cyrenius/Quirinius

Earlier we quoted some of the discoveries and deductions made by Sir William Ramsay following his research at Antioch in Syria and the surrounding region. Much has been written in attempts to show that Ramsay's conclusions were incorrect. He may have silenced earlier critics, but others have since arisen.

There is still dispute over the governorship of Cyrenius (or Quirinius as most sources call him). However it is a problem of *silence* amongst the non-biblical records and thus remains a matter to be cleared up by future archaeological research. The fact is that his governorship of Syria at the time mentioned in Luke 2:1-5 is not recorded in any existing document relating to the reign of Caesar Augustus. Thus critics like George Ogg, in *The Expository Times,* conclude that Luke got it wrong; whereas G. B. Caird in *The Interpreter's Dictionary of the Bible,* Ethelbert Stauffer in *Jesus and His Story,* and Merril F. Unger in *Archaeology of the Old Testament,* as well as Ramsay in *Was Christ born at Bethlehem,* all defend Luke's account.

It is certain that Quirinius was a distinguished soldier and statesman during the period Luke wrote about, and thus there is no reason at all why he should not have been put in charge of the taxing/registration mentioned in Luke 2:1-5. Such a registration could possibly have extended over a period of ten years or more, and thus may not have been completed until about AD 6, when it is known that Quirinius was governor of Syria. However, as this is still an issue of debate amongst some people, we shall go into this problem again dealing with it a little more fully. According to Luke 2:1-5, the taxing or registration which occurred at the time of the birth of the Lord Jesus Christ was the first, or at least, the first of its kind, to be made when Quirinius was governor of

Syria. This has provoked must writing in judgment of, and then much in defence of, Luke's reliability as an historian. The critics have questioned Luke's account on the following points:

(1) There is no record outside of the Bible that Caesar Augustus ordered a registration in the Roman world, as implied by Luke, and there is not even any likelihood that such a registration would have been required.

(2) Know sources seem to indicate that the governors of Syria were as follows:
    9-6 BC C. Sentius Saturninus
    6-4 BC P. Quintilius Varus
Thus there appears to be no room for P. Sulpicius Quirinius at the required time.

(3) It is known that Quirinius was governor of Syria in AD 6, and that at that time a registration was held which included both Syria and the newly formed province of Judea.

In the light of these points George Ogg argues that Luke either dated Christ's birth incorrectly, or had confused the registration in AD 6 with an earlier one at the time of Christ's birth. Can these objections be answered? Earlier we answered some of these points, but now we go into more details giving other views.

(1) Caird point out that Luke does not claim that Caesar Augustus inaugurated a single, uniform registration of the whole Roman world. "All he [Luke] says is that Augustus issued a decree that there should be regular enrolments of the provincials, just as there had always been regular enrolments of Roman citizens." Thus the first criticism arises from reading into the text something which isn't there.

(2) Ramsay, Stauffer and Unger indicate that it was probable that Quirinius held, alongside the governorship of Syria, a special command in relation to the registration, and he had even wider responsibilities. Ramsay shows that, at that time, Varus was

controlling the internal affairs of Syria, but Quirinius was directing its armies and foreign policies. After the Homanadensian War 12-6 BC, which Quirinius had commanded as legate of Syria, he was then free to take up other duties; and thus the registration could easily have been one of them. What the exact relationship was between Varus and Quirinius, only future archaeological discoveries may answer.

(3) The reign of Caesar Augustus was poorly documented; and the silence of the secular ancient records over the issue of Quirinius's governorship is not weighty evidence against Luke. In fact Luke knew about the registration of AD 6, which provoked the uprising of Judas the Galilean, for he wrote about it in Acts 5:37. Thus in Luke 2:1-5 he is careful to distinguish the registration at the time of Christ's birth from that later one. That is the mark of a careful, reliable historian.

Earlier we stated how the absence of non-biblical archaeological records can never be taken as proof of biblical error. The problem of Quirinius and Syria is to do with the poor documentation of the reign of Caesar Augustus. Unger states that the problem remains to be cleared up by further archaeological research. The crux of the problem is to fit Quirinius's governorship of Syria into the years before 4 BC.

It is known that Quirinius began to govern Syria in about AD 6, and this is connected with Coponius' procuratorship of Judea (Josephus, *Antiquities* 18, 1, 1). Also Josephus dates the registration conducted by Quirinius as 37 years after Caesar's victory at Actium, which took place in 31 BC. Thus the date would be AD 6 (*Antiquities* 18, 2, 1), but a registration in the years AD 6/7 would be too late to be related to the birth of Christ. Thus there must have been an earlier registration.

The problem can be solved by associating Quirinius with the governorship of Syria *twice*. In Titulus Tiburtinus The inscription 'Return Syrium', i.e. 'a second time to Syria', was taken by Ramsay to refer to Quirinius. Certainly there is evidence to show that Quirinius started a governorship of Syria in about AD 6, but there is also evidence to show that he was associated with that region twelve or more years earlier. For example, an inscription, discovered at Antioch in Pisidia, and dated 10-7 BC, refers to Gaius Coristanius Fronto as 'prefect of P. Sulpicius Quirinius duumvir'.

Another inscription discovered in a village close to Antioch mentions this same man, Gaius Coristanius Fronto, as 'prefect to P. Sulp. Quirinius duumvir' and also as 'prefect to M. Servilius'. The word 'duumvir' means praetor which originally was used of a Roman consul as leader of the army. Later it referred to the annually elected magistrate performing some of the duties of the consul. Loosely it meant governor; and Ramsay was led to conclude that Quirinius and Servilius were governing the two adjoining provinces of Syria – Cilicia and Galatia round about 8 BC, before the registration of Luke 2:2 was made.

The evidence points towards two registrations and to Quirinius being twice associated with the governorship of Syria.

Appendix 3:
More details of scientific organizations which uphold belief in Divine Creation

As well as the Creation Research Society of the USA., which publishes a *Quarterly Journal,* we should mention three British *scientific* societies dedicated to research into the truth of creation. They are:

(1) The Biblical Creation Society, at **www.biblicalcreation.org.uk**, which holds many one-day conferences in London, and publishes the papers presented at those conferences.

(2) The Newton Scientific Association (no known website or contact details) which published such small gems as *Mathematical Problems in the Evolutionary Model*, by Dr. Stephen W. Ellacott.

(3) Creation Science Ministries (at **http://www.csm.org.uk,** formerly the Evolution Protest Movement, 1932-1972); which publishes the *Creation Journal* as well as a wide range of pamphlets (such as *Scientists Critical of Evolution* by Dr. D. T. Rosevear), and books (such as *Fossil Man: A Re-Appraisal* by F. W. Cousins).

In the USA, much has been heard more recently about *Intelligent Design* (**www.uncommondescent.com**); and more of their position can be learnt from that website

Also in the USA is the organization *Reasons to Believe,* spearheaded by Hugh Ross, which upholds the view of progressive divine creation.

There are also a number of other groups which can be contacted from their websites, such as:

- **www.answersingenesis.org**
- **www.creation.com**
- **www.biblicalcreationministries.org.uk**
- **www.creation.com**

The organisation may well have different interpretations of Genesis 1 and have different understandings of how God created. However, they all contain scientists who have ***not*** been convinced by atheistic evolution. We have given this information just to show that the idea that 'evolution has been proved beyond doubt' is not accepted in all scientific circles and by all scientists. The popular press and the media may treat it as such, but those who disagree are given little or no coverage.

Appendix 4: Some of the Prophecies relating to the Lord Jesus Christ

The initial title of this appendix was *'Fifty* Prophecies Relating to the Lord Jesus Christ', but as the work progressed it got changed to *'Over Fifty* Prophecies!'* At a later stage it was changed yet again to *Sixty* Prophecies!!', and now we have settled on the above title because what follows is not an exhaustive list. No doubt many more could be added, and the reader may care to compile his own list of additions.

Please note that in what follows we have, in general, given in each case just *one* Old Testament prophecy/prediction and just *one* New Testament record of its fulfilment. However we should point out that in the majority of cases the same or similar prophecy occurs in other places in the Old Testament, and that other accounts of the fulfilment are recorded in other books of the New Testament. We have kept, in general, to one book from each Testament in order to save space.

A.   *Events surrounding the birth of the Lord Jesus Christ*

The prophecy	OT prediction	NT fulfilment
1. Christ's pre-existence	Ps. 102:25 Isa 9:6-7; 41:4; 44:6; Micah 5:2	John 1:1-2; 8:58; 17:5,24; Col 1:17; Rev 1:17; 2:8; 22:13
2. Christ ... The Son of God	1 Chron 17:11-14; 2 Sam 7:12-16; Ps 2:7	Matt 3:17; 16:16; Luke 9:35; 22:70; John 1:34, 49
3. The Son of	Gen 12:2-3; 22:18	Matt 1:1;

Abraham		Gal 3:16
4. The Son of Isaac	Gen 21:12	Matt 1:2; Luke 3:23-24
5. The Son of Jacob	Gen 35:10-12; Num 24:17	Matt 1:2; Luke 1:33; 3:23,34
6. The Son of Judah	Gen 49:10 Micah 5:2	Luke 3:23,30 Heb 7:14
7. The Son of Jesse	Isa 11:1, 10	Luke 3:23, 32
8. The Son of David	2 Sam 7:12, 16	Matt 1:1
9. Born of a virgin	Isa 7:14	Matt 1:18, 24-25 Luke 1:26-35
10. Seed of woman	Gen 3:15	Matt 1:20; Gal 4:4
11. House of David	Jer 23:5 Ps 132:11	Luke 3:23, 31 Acts 13:22-23
12. Born at Bethlehem	Micah 5:2	Matt 2:1,6
13. To be called Immanuel	Isa 7:14	Matt 1:23
14. To be called Lord	Ps 110:1 Jer 23:6	Luke 2:11 Luke 20:28
15. To be given gifts	Ps 72:10-15	Matt 2:1,11
16. Herod to kill the children	Jer 31:15	Matt 2:16

B. Events surrounding the life of the Lord Jesus Christ

The prophecy	OT prediction	NT fulfilment
17. Christ-preceded by the messenger	Isa 40:3 Mal 3:1	Matt 3:1-3; 11:10; John 1:23
18. –specially anointed by the Holy Spirit	Psa 45:7; Isa 11:2; 42:1; 61:1-2	Matt 3:16-17; 12:17-21; John 1:32
19. Christ's ministry- to start in Galilee	Isa 9:1	Matt 4:12-17
20. –of miracles	Isa 32:3-4; 35:5-6	Matt 9:32-35; 11:4-6

21. –of parables	Ps 78:2	Matt 13:3,10,34
22. Christ–The Prophet	Deut 18:18	Matt 21:11
23. – The Priest	Ps 110:4	Matt 21:5; 27:37; John 18:33-35
24. – The King	Ps 2:6 Zech 9:9	Matt 21:5; 27:37 John 18:33-35
25. – The Judge	Isa 33:22	John 5:30
26. Christ –to enter Jerusalem on a donkey	Zech 9:9	Matt 21:6-11 Luke 19:30-38
27. – to enter the Temple	Mal 3:1	Matt 21:12
28. – to have zeal for God	Ps 69:9	John 12:15-17
29. – to be rejected by his own people	Ps 69:8; 118:22; Isa 53:3	Matt 21:42-43 John 1:11; 7:5,48
30. – to be hated without a cause	Ps 69:4	John 15:25
31. – to be a stumbling stone to the Jews	Ps 118:22; Isa 8:14; 28:16	Rom 8:32-33 1 Peter 2:7

C. Events surrounding the death of the Lord Jesus Christ

The prophecy	OT prediction	NT fulfilment
32. Betrayed by a friend	Ps 41:9; 55:12-14	Matt 10:4; 26:48-50; John 13:21
33. Sold for 30 pieces of silver	Zech 11:12	Matt 26:15; 27:3
34. That money-thrown in the temple	Zech 11:13	Matt 27:5
35. – bought the potter's field	Zech 11:13	Matt 27:7

36. Forsaken by his disciples	Zech 13:7	Matt 26:31 Mark 14:27,50
37. Accused by false witnesses	Ps 35:11	Matt 26:57-61
38. Beaten and spat upon	Isa 50:6 Micah 5:1	Matt 26:67 Luke 22:63
39. Wounded and-bruised	Isa 53:5	Matt 27:30
40. To remain dumb	Isa 53:7	Matt 27:12-19
41. To be mocked	Ps 22:7-8	Matt 27:31
42. To fall under the cross	Ps 109:24-25	Matt 27:31-32; Mark 15:21; Luke 25:26
43. Crucified with thieves	Isa 53:12	Matt 27:38
44. His hands and feet pierced	Ps 22:16 Zech 12:10	Luke 23:33 John 20:25
45. Prayed for his persecutors	Isa 53:12	Luke 23:34
46. The people stared at him	Ps 22:17	Luke 23:35
47. They shook their heads	Ps 109:25	Matt 27:39
48. They ridiculed him	Ps 22:7-8	Matt 27:41-43
49. He bare the sins of many	Isa 53:12	2 Cor 5:21
50. Darkness over the land	Amos 8:9	Matt 27:45
51. His garments were parted	Ps 22:18	John 19:23-24
52. Lots cast for his tunic	Ps 22:18	John 19:23-24
53. He suffered thirst	Ps 69:21	John 19:28
54. Given gall and vinegar to drink	Ps 69:21	John 19:28-29
55. The cry!	Ps 22:1	Matt 27:46
56.He committed himself to God	Ps 31:5	Luke 23:46

57. His friends stood afar off	Ps 38:11	Luke 23:49
58. No bones broken	Ps 34:20	John 19:33
59. His side pierced	Zech 12:10	John 19:34
60. A broken heart	Ps 22:14	John 19:34
61. Buried in a rich man's tomb	Isa 53:9	Matt 27:57-60
62. The resurrection	Ps 16:10;30:3 41:10; Hos 6:2	Matt 28:6;Mark 16:6;Luke 24:46;Acts 2:31;1 Cor 15:1-8
63. The ascension	Ps 68:18	Acts 1:9
64. Seated on the right hand of God	Ps 110:1	Heb 1:3

Appendix 5: The Structure of the Eight Signs of John's Gospel

Appendix 176 of *The Companion Bible* gives the following structure for the signs in John's Gospel, John 2:1-11 ... 21:1-4.

THE EIGHT SIGNS IN JOHN'S GOSPEL

A 2:1-11 The marriage in Cana
   B 4:46-52 The ruler's son
      C 5:1-47 The impotent man
         D 6:1-14 The feeding of the five thousand
         D 6:15-21 The walking on the sea
      C 9:1-41 The man born blind
   B 11:1-44 The sisters' brother
A 21:1-14 The draught of fishes

Further symmetry can be seen in the detail of each pair of signs.

A. 2:1-11. **The marriage in Cana**
    The background. Nathanael's faith (1:49-51).
      The Place. Galilee (v 1).
        'The third day' (v 1).
          Wine provided (v 8, 9).
            'Jesus was called, and his disciples' (v 2).
              Failure confessed. 'They have no wine (v 3).
                Numbers 6 waterpots, holding 2-3 firkins each
                (v 6).
                  Command.'Fill the waterpots with water' (v-
                  7)
                    Obedience. 'They filled them' (v-7-).
                    Waterpots filled. 'Up to the brim'(v-
                    7).
                      The servants bare (v 8).
                      Glory manifested (v 11-).
                      His disciples' faith (v-11).

A 21:1-14. **The draught of fishes**
    The background. Thomas's unbelief (20:24-29).
      The Place. Galilee (v 1).
        'The third time' (v 14).
          A meal provided (v 9).
            The Lord was the Caller of his disciples (vv 5,12).
              Failure confessed. They had 'caught nothing' (v 3).
              Had 'no meat' (v 5).
                Numbers: 200 cubits (v 8); 153 fishes (v 11).
                  Command 'Cast the net into the water'(v 6).
                  Obedience. 'They cast therefore' (v 6).
                Net full, to the last fish (vv 8, 11).
                  'Bring of the fish' (v 10).
                    The Lord manifested (v 14).
                      His disciples' love (vv 15-17).

B 4:46-52. **The ruler's son**
The background. Rejection (vv 43, 44).
   Time. After two days' (v 43).
      His son. 'Sick' (v 46).
         Parenthetic explanation *re* the place (Cana) (v 46).
            'At the point of death'(v 47).'Death'only here, and in "*B'*.
               'Ye will not believe' (v 48).
                  'Ere my child die' (v 49).
                     The servants 'met him' (v 51).
                        'Thy son liveth' (v 51).
                           'The fever left him' (v 52).

B 11:1-44. **The sisters' brother**
The background. Rejection (10:31, 39; 11:8).
   Time. 'Jesus abode two days where he was' (v 6).
      'Lazarus was sick' (v 2).
         Parenthetic explanations *re* the person (Mary) (v 2).
            'Lazarus is dead' (v 14). 'Death' only here, and in 'B'.
               'That ye may believe' (v 15).
                  'Our brother had not died' (vv 21,32).
                     Martha 'met him' (vv 20, 30).
                        'Lazarus, come forth' (v 43).
                         'Let him go' (v 44).

C 5:1-47. **The impotent man**

  The Place. Jerusalem (v 1).

    The Pool. Bethesda (v 2).

      The longstanding case, 'thirty-eight years' (v 5).

        'Jesus saw him' (v 6).

          The Lord takes the initiative (v 6).

            'The same day was the Sabbath' (v 9).

              'Afterward Jesus findeth him' (v 14).

                'Sin no more'(v 14). 'Sin' only here and in '*C*'.

                  'My Father worketh hitherto, and I work' (v 17).

                    A double reference to 'Moses' (vv 45, 46).

C 9:1-41. **The man born blind**

  The Place. Jerusalem (8:59; 9:1).

    The Pool. Siloam (vv 7,11).

      The longstanding case, "from birth" (v 1).

        'Jesus saw' him (v 1).

          The Lord takes the initiative (v 6).

            'It was the Sabbath day' (v 14).

              'When he had found him' (v 35).

                'Who did sin?' (v 2 Cp. vv 24, 25, 31, 34).

                'Sin' only here, and in 'C'.

                  'I must work the works of him that sent Me' (v 4).

                    A double reference to 'Moses' (vv 28, 29).

D 6:1-14. **The feeding of the five thousand**
  The only 'sign' (with *D*) recorded in the other Gospels (Matt 14:15
  Mark 6:35 Luke 9:10).
      'Jesus went up into the mountain' (v 3).
          Followed by a discourse (vv 26-65). Signification.
              'Many disciples went back' (v 66).
                  The testimony of Peter (vv 68, 69).

D 6:15-21. **The walking on the sea**
  The only 'sign' (with D) recorded in the other Gospels
  (Matt 14:23 Mark 6:47).
      'Jesus departed again into the mountain' (v 15).
          Followed by a discourse (ch 7). Signification.
              'Many of the people believed' (7:31).
                  The testimony of Nicodemus (7:50).

Appendix 6:
The Structure of
Ephesians: (1:3-3:13;
3:14-21; 4:1-6:24)

Ephesians must have been quite a headache for Paul to plan, if he did plan it, for the epistle contains fifteen groups of three. The whole book, apart from the salutation and doxology, is based on threes. (The following is taken from *In Heavenly Places* by Charles H. Welch.)

THE DOCTRINAL SECTIONS (1:3-3:13)
(1) The threefold charter (1:3-14).
> (a) The will of the Father.
> (b) The work of the Son.
> (c) The witness of the Spirit.

(2) The threefold prayer (1:15-19)
> (a) That ye may know what is the hope of his calling.
> (b) That ye may know what are the riches of the glory of his inheritance in the saints.
> (c) That ye may know what is the exceeding greatness of his power toward us who believe.

(3) The threefold fellowship (1:19-2:7)
> (a) Quickened together with Christ.
> (b) Raised together.
> (c) Made us sit together in heavenly places in Christ Jesus.

(4) The three works (2:8-10)
> (a) Not of works, lest any man should boast.
> (b) We are his workmanship.
> (c) Created in Christ Jesus unto good works.

(5) The threefold peace (2:11-19a)
> (a) Far off are made nigh . . . He is our peace.

(b) Of the two a new man created, so making peace.

(c) Reconciliation and access. He came and preached peace to those that were far off, and to those that were nigh.

(6) The threefold fellowship (2:19b-22)

(a) No more strangers but *fellow* citizens.

(b) The whole building fitly framed *together.*

(c) Builded *together* for an habitation of God.

(7) The threefold equality (3:1-13)

(a) In spirit the Gentiles are heirs on an equality.

(b) They are members of a body, all on perfect equality.

(c) They are partakers in the promise of Christ by the gospel entrusted to Paul, on an equality.

THE CENTRAL PRAYER (Ephesians 3:14-21)

The threefold prayer (3:14-21)

(a) In order that he would grant you to be strengthened.

(b) In order that ye may be able to comprehend.

(c) In order that ye might be filled unto all fullness of God.

THE PRACTICAL SECTION (Ephesians 4:1-6:24)

(1) The threefold exhortation (4:1-6)

(a) Walk worthy of the calling.

(b) Forbear one another in love.

(c) Endeavour to keep the unity of the Spirit.

(2) A threefold measure (4:7-19)

(a) The measure of the gift of Christ

(b) The measure of the fullness of Christ.

(c) The measure of every part.

(3) A threefold application of the truth 'in Jesus' (4:20-32)

(a) Put off the old man, concerning the former conversation.

(b) Put on the new man which is created in righteousness.

(c) Put away the lie, speak every man truth.

(4) A threefold walk (5:1-6:9)

(a) Walk in love. WIVES AND HUSBANDS.

(b) Walk in light. CHILDREN AND PARENTS.

(c) Walk circumspectly. SERVANTS AND MASTERS.

(5) A threefold stand (6:10-13)

(a) Put on the whole armour of God, that ye may be able to stand against the wiles of the Devil.

(b) Take unto you the whole armour of God, that ye may be able to withstand in the evil day.

(c) And having 'worked out' all, to stand.

(6) A threefold equipment (6:14-18)

(a) GIRDLE of Truth and BREASTPLATE of Righteousness.

(b) SHOES of Peace and SHIELD of Faith.

(c) HELMET of Salvation and SWORD of the Spirit.

(7) A threefold prayer for utterance (6:19-20)

(a) That I may open my mouth boldly.

(b) That therein I may speak boldly.

(c) As I ought to speak.

We ask our readers to consider, again, the above in detail so that they can see how impossible it would be sit down and design a letter with that format, unless the Spirit of God was guiding you.

Appendix 7: Number of earth-quakes each year

Appendix 7: Number of earthquakes each year 1970-2010

The data is from the United States Geological Survey to 7 November 2010

year	number of earthquakes in magnitude range					estimated deaths
	8.0 to 9.9	7.0 to 7.9	6.0 to 6.9	5.0 to 5.9	5.0 to 9.9	
1970	0	20	110	1,195	1,325	68,202
1971	1	19	112	1,331	1,463	1,279
1972	0	15	110	1,316	1,441	11,179
1973	0	13	95	1,331	1,439	659
1974	0	14	99	1,312	1,425	5,440
1975	1	14	107	1,447	1,569	12,372
1976	2	15	114	1,649	1,780	697,309
1977	2	11	89	1,686	1,788	2,849
1978	0	16	93	1,526	1,635	15,192
1979	0	13	100	1,366	1,479	1,475
1980	1	13	105	1,299	1,418	8,620
1981	0	13	90	1,168	1,271	5,223
1982	0	10	85	1,425	1,520	3,328
1983	0	14	126	1,673	1,813	2,372
1984	0	8	91	1,579	1,678	174
1985	1	13	110	1,674	1,798	9,846

1986	1	5	89	1,665	1,760	1,068
1987	0	11	112	1,437	1,560	1,080
1988	0	8	93	1,485	1,586	26,552
1989	1	6	79	1,444	1,530	617
1990	0	18	109	1,617	1,744	52,056
1991	0	16	96	1,457	1,569	3,210
1992	0	13	166	1,498	1,677	3,920
1993	0	12	137	1,426	1,575	10,096
1994	2	11	146	1,542	1,701	1,634
1995	2	18	183	1,318	1,521	7,980
1996	1	14	149	1,222	1,386	589
1997	0	16	120	1,113	1,249	3,069
1998	1	11	117	979	1,108	9,430
1999	0	18	116	1,104	1,238	22,662
2000	1	14	146	1,344	1,505	231
2001	1	15	121	1,224	1,361	21,357
2002	0	13	127	1,201	1,341	1,685
2003	1	14	140	1,203	1,358	33,819
2004	2	14	141	1,515	1,672	228,802
2005	1	10	140	1,693	1,844	82,364
2006	2	9	142	1,712	1,865	6,605

2007	4	14	178	2,074	2,270	712
2008	0	12	168	1,768	1,948	88,011
2009	1	16	141	1,872	2,030	1,787
2010	1	19	135	1,547	1,702	226,668

The data for 2010 is not for the full year; figures published 7 November

Books quoted or referred to

(Both directly and indirectly, including in Footnotes)

Allen, Stuart	*The Unfolding Purpose of God*
Allen, Stuart & Welch, C. H.	*Perfection or Perdition*
Anderson, Sir Robert	*Daniel in the Critics' Den*
Attenborough, Richard	'evolution has been proved beyond doubt ...
Archer, Gleason	*A Survey of the Old Testament*
BBC Radio 4	Giantism
Beverley, Marcus	*The Christian Herald*
Boyd, Robert	'a poem entitled *Creation* ...
	"The mystery of being ...
Bradlaugh, Charles	
British Museum, The	'the papyri discovered in Egypt'; etc.
Bruce F. F.	*The Book and the Parchments*
	The New Testament Documents
Bullinger, E. W.	*Number in Scripture*
	The Companion Bible: Preface
	(CB:) Appendices 50,30;10;176
Burrows, Max	*What Mean these Stones?*
Butler, Samuel	"Books should be tried by a and ...
Caird, G. B.	*The Interpreter's Dictionary of the Bible*
	"All he [Luke] says is that Augustus ...
Chamfort, Nicholas	"Most contemporary books ...
Charon, Dr. Jean	*Cosmology*; "who created the world? ...
Colton, Charles Caleb	"Many books require no thought ...
Cousins, F. W.	*Fossil Man: A Re-Appraisal;* CSM
Coverdale, Miles	"It shall greatly helpe ye to understande ...
Creation Science Ministries	*Creation Journal*
Creation Research Society	*Quarterly Journal*

Custance, Arthur	*Doorway Paper 'Who taught Adam to speak?'*
Davidson, Samuel	*The Hebrew Text of the Old Testament*
Dawkins, Richard	'evolution...proved beyond doubt ...
de Morgan, M. J.	'the Code of Hammurabi ...
Deyo, Stan	*Cosmic Conspiracy*
Dickens, Charles	"There are books of which the backs ...
Ellacott, Dr. Stephen W.	*Mathematical Problems in the Evolutionary Model*
Evans, Sir Arthur	'the Minoan Civilisation based on Crete ...
France, Anatole	"Never lend books, ... "The books that everybody admires ...
Free, Joseph	*Archaeology and Bible History*
Gallant, René	*Bombarded Earth*
Garstang, Prof. John	*Joshua and Judges*
Geisler and Nix	*A General Introduction to the Bible*
Gladstone, W. E.	"...I will back the masses, ... "Bible ... 'the impregnable rock ...
Goldman, James	*The Lion in Winter* *Myself as Witness*
Guardian Weekly, The	Science is not value free
Heine, Heinrich	"I fell asleep reading a dull book, ...
Homer	*Iliad*
Huxley, Aldous	"I had motives for ... [*the Report*, June 1966]
Josephus	*Antiquities of the Jews*
Julius Caesar	*Gallic War*
Keller, Werner	*The Bible as History*
Kenyon, Sir Frederick	*Our Bible and the Ancient Manuscripts*
Keyes, Sydney	*The Kestrel.* "...no virtue ... in blind reliance ...
Langdon, Dr. Stephen	"In this layer [at Kish] ...Letter to The Times "A flood over that part of Mesopotamia ...
Lightfoot, Bishop	"If we could only recover ...
Livy	*Roman History*
Mail, the	"the skeleton of Charles Byrne, ...
Masson, Tom	"there are seventy million books ...
Mencken, H. L.	"In the main there are two sorts of book, ... "The chief knowledge that a man gets ...

Metzger, Bruce	Iliad and Mhabharata data
Mill, John Stuart	Letter to his father
Montgomery, J. W.	*History and Christianity*
Moore, George	"If good books did good ...
Noorbergen, Rend	*Secrets of the Lost Races*
Ogg, George	*The Expository Times*
Ozanne, Charles R.	*The First 7,000 years,* Appendix 1; incl. analysis of 'the first chapter of Genesis'
Panin, Ivan	*The Inspiration of Scriptures Scientifically Demonstrated,* [the 'New York Sun letter'. Matthew 1; etc.] *The Numeric Greek New Testament*
Penny, Michael	*40 Problem Passages* *Approaching the Bible* OBT *The Existence of Christ,* OBT (free download **www.obt.org.uk**) *The Manual on the Gospel of John,* OBT
Penny, Michael & Sylvia	*Introducing God's Plan,* OBT
Penny, Sylvia	*Noah's Flood,* OBT *Theories of Creation,* OBT
Phillips, J. B.	*Your God is Too Small* *Republic*
Pliny the Younger	*History*
Porter, Rev. J. L.	*The Giant Cities of Bashan*
Ramsay, Sir William M.	'a block of stone bearing a Latin ... "If an author can be guilty of ..." *Was Christ born at Bethlehem?*
Readers Digest	*Readers Digest Atlas*
Robertson, A. T.	*An Introduction to Textual Criticism of the New Testament*
Roche, James Jeffrey	"Some men borrow books, some men steal ...
Rosevear, Dr. D. T.	*Scientists Critical of Evolution;* CSM
Ross, Hugh	Reasons to Believe
Russell, Bertrand	"If we could all learn to love our neighbor ...
Scott, Sir Walter	"Please return this book ...
Scroggie, Graham	*The Unfolding Drama of Redemption*
Stauffer, Ethelbert	*Jesus and His Story*

Stoner, Peter	*Science Speaks: An Evaluation of Certain Christian Evidences*
Stoppard, Tom	*Jumpers*
Suetonius	*De Vita Caesarum*
Tacitus	*Annals*
Tennyson	*This better to have loved and lost,*
Uncommon Descent website	"Uncommon Descent holds that ...
Unger, Merril F.	*Archaeology of the Old Testament*
Velikovsky, Immanuel	*Earth in Upheaval*
	Worlds in Collision
Vos, Howard	*Can I Trust the Bible?*
Warfield, Benjamin	*Introduction to Textual Criticism of the New Testament*
Watson, David	*Myths and Miracles*
Welch C. H.	*In Heavenly Places:* [Ephesians]
	The Volume of the Book
	True from the Beginning
	Perfection or Perdition?; [Hebrews]
[Allen, Stuart; & ...]	[see above, under Allen, Stuart; ...]
Wellhausan	"We may not regard him as an historical person [Abraham], ...
Whitcomb & Morris	*The Genesis Flood*
Wiseman, D. J.	*Illustrations of Old Testament History*
Wiseman, P. J.	*Creation revealed in Six Days*
Wooley, Dr. C. L.	"The shafts ...[at Ur of the Chaldees]
	"The Sumerians ... [Letter to The Times]
Yahuda, Dr. A. S.	*The Language of the Pentateuch in its Relation to Egypt*
Young, Robert	*Young's Literal Translation* [of the Bible]

Also

Assumption of Moses; apocryphal
Book of Enoch; apocryphal
Encyclopedia Britannica
Mahabharata; the national epic of India
New Bible Dictionary, 2nd edition, page 81,
The Bible, designed to be Read as Literature
The Englishman's Greek New Testament
The Massorah
The Oxford Dictionary
United States Geological Survey

———————————————

Publications of The Open Bible Trust must be in accordance with its evangelical, fundamental and dispensational basis. However, beyond this minimum, writers are free to express whatever beliefs they may have as their own understanding, provided that the aim in so doing is to further the object of The Open Bible Trust. A copy of the doctrinal basis is available on **www.obt.org.uk** and from:

The Open Bible Trust
Fordland Mount, Upper Basildon,
Reading, RG8 8LU, UK.

About the Author

Michael Penny was born in Ebbw Vale, Gwent, Wales, in 1943. He read Mathematics at the University of Reading, before teaching for twelve years and becoming the Director of Mathematics and Business Studies at Queen Mary's College Basingstoke in Hampshire, England. In 1978 he entered Christian publishing, and in 1984 became the administrator of The Open Bible Trust.

He held this position for seven years, before moving to the USA and becoming pastor of Grace Church in New Berlin, Wisconsin. He returned to Britain in 1999, and is at present the Administrator and Editor of The Open Bible Trust. In 2010 he was elected Chairman of Churches Together in Reading, where he speaks in a number of churches of different denominations. He is also a member of the Advisory Committee to Reading University Christian Union and a chaplain at Reading College. He lives near Reading with his wife and has appeared on Premier Radio and BBC Radio Berkshire many times. He has made several speaking tours of America, Canada, Australia, New Zealand and the Netherlands, as well as others to South Africa and the Philippines. Some of his writings have been translated into German and Russian.

He has written over 50 books– including *40 Problems Passages, Galatians: Interpretation and Application, Joel's Prophecy: Past and Future, Approaching the Bible, The Miracles of the Apostles*.

Further details of these, and his other publications, can be seen on

www.obt.org.uk/michael-penny

The above are available as both perfect bound books (from the Open Bible Trust) and eBooks (from Amazon Kindle and Apple), and as KDP paperbacks from Amazon.

Michael Penny is editor of *Search* magazine

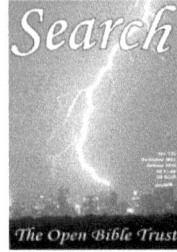

For a free sample of
The Open Bible Trust's magazine *Search*,
please email

admin@obt.org.uk

or visit

www.obt.org.uk/search

Also by Michael Penny

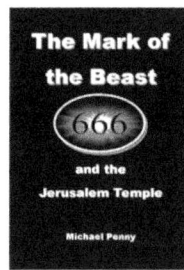

The Miracles of the Apostles – details on the next page
A Key to Unfulfilled Prophecy
Approaching the Bible
The Mark of the Beast and the Jerusalem Temple

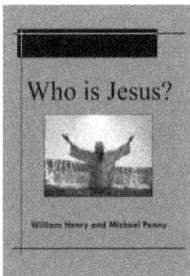

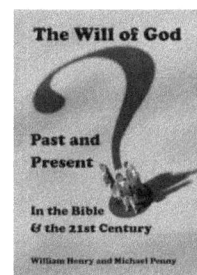

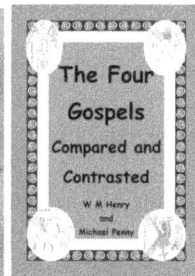

These four books were written with W M Henry
Who is Jesus?
Following Philippians
The Will of God: Past and Present
The Four Gospels: Compared and Contrasted

Details are available on www.obt.org.uk

Copies can be ordered from that website.

They are also available as eBooks from Amazon and Apple
and as KDP paperbacks from Amazon

The Miracles of the Apostles
Michael Penny

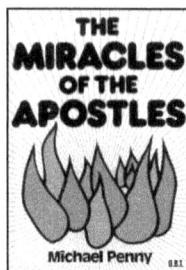

The Acts of the Apostles covers one of the most dramatic stages in God's plan for the people of Israel. They had rejected their Messiah with cries of "Crucify Him! Crucify Him!", but He had prayed "Father, forgive them, for they do not know what they are doing." That prayer was answered because it was through ignorance that both the common people and their leaders turned their backs upon Jesus and under the Mosaic Law a person who sinned through ignorance, or unintentionally, could be forgiven.

That being the case, the burning issue for the apostles was to ask the Lord, "Are you at this time going to restore the kingdom to Israel?" but they were not given a direct answer. They were told that "It is not for you to know the times or date the Father has set by his own authority" (Acts 1:6-7). Whether or not that kingdom would be restored to Israel at that time depended upon the response of that nation itself. It would be restored only when the King returned and set up His kingdom. Would He return soon? Would He come back within the lifetime of the apostles? That was the issue and, that, according to Peter, depended upon Israel repenting (Acts 3:19-21).

In order to encourage Israel to repent, and to ensure that they were without excuse if they failed to do so, the apostles were given the power to perform various wonders and signs. These were *The Miracles of the Apostles* and included speaking and interpreting tongues, knowledge and wisdom, healing and judgement, visions and voices, visitation and revelations, wonders in heaven above and signs on the earth beneath. All these and more, are considered in this book which explains the significance and meaning these miracles should have had to the people of Israel.

"Miracles" were also "signs", i.e. they 'signified' something. A fact missed by the Gentiles of New Testament times, and missed by many Christians today.

This book explains the significance of each and every type of miracle performed by the Apostles.

Further details on www.obt.org.uk

www.ingramcontent.com/pod-product-compliance
Lightning Source LLC
Chambersburg PA
CBHW071532040426
42452CB00008B/983